It is great to see that Dermot has finally published a book! His ability to help individuals and teams transform their work practices is second to none!

— **Ed Box**, Banking and Finance Executive

I first met Dermot in 2002. At that time Dermot was an expert in managing time and priorities using a paper-based system. Over the years Dermot has evolved into the leading coach in utilising devices, Microsoft Office and systems to manage time and priorities. Thirteen years after first meeting Dermot I still use his principles and we use him in coaching our teams to become more effective. The skills Dermot teaches are life changing and I have no hesitation in endorsing Dermot and this book.

— **Scott Boyes**, Vice President Operations,
Accor Hotels

Smart Work is the upgrade we needed to have. Triage your life and read this book.

— **Matt Church**, Founder,
Thought Leaders Global and author of *Amplifiers*

Learning to work productively in the digital age is the critical business challenge of our time. Dermot Crowley has taken a seemingly insurmountable problem, distilled it down to three key concepts, and provided a step-by-step process to revolutionise productivity. What David Allen's *Getting Things Done* did for the noughties, *Smart Work* is set to do for our technology-driven time. Dermot's work has had a profound impact on me and my team, and transformed not only the way we work, but also what we even consider possible. If you want to achieve more, stress less, and spend more of your day doing work that matters, *Smart Work* is for you.

— **Peter Cook**, author of *The New Rules of Management*

The brilliance of the techniques that Dermot teaches is that they are so simple—and yet so incredibly effective. Anyone who has ever felt overwhelmed by the sheer volume of information in their daily workload should read this book.

— **Nick Dempsey**, Head of FICC Compliance, Macquarie Bank

If you have ever answered 'Busy' to the question 'How are you?' then this book is for you. Dermot provides insights, solutions and practical tips for anyone who needs to manage their time, technology and energy better. In an age where we are constantly asked to work smarter . . . *Smart Work* shows us how.

— **Gabrielle Dolan**, author of *Ignite*

Smart Work is a great read for any busy executive who is struggling to stay focused on the important work in a workplace driven by urgency, meetings and emails. Dermot's approach to productivity is practical, relevant and smart.

— **Susan Ferrier**, National Managing Partner, People, Performance & Culture, KPMG

Dermot's work is magic. The ideas in this book will add hours to your day and weeks to your year. So! Liberate yourself from draining, dumb and defunct ways of working—discover how to work smart today.

— **Dr Jason Fox**, motivational scientist and author of *The Game Changer* and *How to Lead a Quest*

They used to say 'If you want something done, give it to a busy person'. In my opinion, this maxim should read, 'If you want something done, give it to Dermot Crowley'. Dermot is, without question, the master of productivity and doing what works.

— **Dan Gregory**, CEO, The Impossible Institute and co-author of *Selfish, Scared & Stupid*

Life is as busy as it has ever been. Effort is key, but time is of the essence. We have to adapt, we have to improve, we have to be more efficient and work smarter. Dermot Crowley is Australia's thought leader on this extremely important subject — working smarter. He has positively impacted captains of industry, executives, executive assistants, and so many other people in so many ways, enabling them to simply focus on what's important and to have a lasting impact. This book will enable and guide you to do exactly that.

— **John Karagounis**, Managing Director and CEO,
The CEO Circle

This is a very simple, easy to follow book that promotes great productivity tips beyond the high level concepts by providing practical day-to-day recommendations that integrate into the tools that we use all day, every day. Well worth the read!

— **Caleb Reeves**, General Manager,
Customer programs, Commonwealth Bank of Australia

Dermot helped me make fundamental changes to the way I use technology and organise my time. I always recommend him to people who are looking to become more efficient, effective and productive.

— **Michael Rose**, Chief Executive Partner,
Allens

I have worked with Dermot for over three years. He has been my personal productivity coach and also trained more than 500 people for me. In both my own experience and for many who adopt his ideas there is a big 'ah-ha!' moment which makes you realise you have become a slave to the urgent and have lost sight of the important. Worse still, the tools for your own productivity were in front of you but you see them as the problem and not the solution.

Once you adopt his methods you suddenly feel in control and your stress levels will drop. I have had people tell me 'It saved my life!' as they felt they were drowning at work from information and contact overload. Another moved from 5000 emails in their inbox to having white space in it!

It's not easy as you have to change from old but well established bad habits to new ones. However, with persistence and the odd relapse, I promise these ideas and this book will change your working life.

— **James Sheffield**, Financial Services Executive

Dermot Crowley is one of the most important people that I have met in the last 25 years. This importance has not come from anything specifically that he did, but in the way he empowered me to act in an organised and proactive way each day. Dermot's approach to staying in control of our increasingly complex daily lives through the intelligent use of technology is easily implemented and actually works! I have followed his approach to personal productivity for the majority of my working life and I could simply not imagine working any other way.

If you wish to produce a higher quality more consistently; if you wish to have more time to actually think throughout the day and most importantly; if you wish to have more control over the balance between your work and personal life, then *Smart Work* is a road map to assist you in achieving this and more.

— **John Slack-Smith**, Executive Director and Chief Operating Officer, Harvey Norman

Dermot's book sets the benchmark on how to get the most out of yourself and every day by focusing on the behaviours that are required to build the successful habits that lead to good outcomes—not just the technology. Applying his approach has helped me gain greater control at work, generate better outcomes and create more balance between work and personal goals. I recommend it highly for anyone who is looking to master their agenda and get the absolute most out of their time.

— **Angus Sullivan**, EGM Retail Products & Strategy, Commonwealth Bank of Australia

SMART PRODUCTIVITY

SMART WORK

SMART
PRODUCTIVITY

SMART WORK

How to Increase Productivity Achieve Balance and Reduce Stress

DERMOT CROWLEY

WILEY

Contents

About the author

Dermot Crowley is a productivity author, speaker, trainer and thought leader. He was born in Dublin, Ireland, and moved to Sydney, Australia, in 1993.

He has more than twenty-five years' experience working in the productivity training industry and has run his own business, Adapt Productivity, since 2002.

His passion for helping workers, leaders and teams to work in a more productive and balanced way has led him to work with many leading organisations around the world such as the Commonwealth Bank of Australia, PepsiCo, Walmart, Citi, Westpac, Deloitte, Allens Linklaters, Allianz and KPMG.

Dermot lives with his family in sunny Sydney. When not training or writing, he can be found in the kitchen practising his other passion — cooking.

Acknowledgements

Being the revised and updated edition of *Smart Work*, there are even more people to thank for their hard work and support. There was a raft of people who helped to bring the first edition to life. Many of these people are still my support squad and I thank you all. A few deserve a special call out.

Tony, Matt and Chauntelle are the team that organise and deliver our training for thousands of clients every year. You guys are amazing, loyal and always working to ensure the Smart concepts make a real difference for people. Your support allows me the space to write books like this. Thank you.

To my crew at Thought Leaders, a huge thank you for inspiring me with the quality company I keep. Matt and Lisa continually push my thinking and encourage me to level up. I am so lucky to be in a community that gets me and helps me. Thank you all.

To my family. Vera, I am the luckiest man in the world to have met you and to have built our life together. My son Finn, who was a baby when I first dreamt of writing this book, and is now a man, and my closest friend. My sister Margaret, who always cheers me on from home. I love you all.

And finally, my clients, who buy my books, attend our training and support our boutique business year after year. I get to do the work I love with the people I like every day. Lucky man. Thank you all.

Preface

I started writing the original *Smart Work* draft over seven years ago. How time flies! I believe it has had a huge impact in the workplace, both as a book and a training program. Since it was published in 2016, many tens of thousands of people have been exposed to the Smart Work methodology and are hopefully seeing and feeling the benefits. I have gone on and written two other books in the series since then, *Smart Teams* published in 2018 and *Lead Smart*, published by Wiley in 2023. In the middle I wrote *Urgent!* as a part of a personal odyssey to dial down the unproductive urgency in the modern workplace.

So back to Smart Work — why the need to rewrite something that already works?

Well firstly, when you write a book and then deliver it as a training program over a number of years, your ideas naturally evolve. The conversations you have with clients, the issues that you see in their workplaces and the insights that you make when delivering content like this shape new thoughts and ideas. It felt like a great opportunity to refresh content that is still relevant, but make it even more relevant with fresh ideas and strategies.

But the big driver for me has been the shift in our workplaces over the past few years. In 2020, COVID blindsided us and changed how we work and live. We have all gone through this together and, at least at the time of writing this, are still going through it together. We can all remember those first few weeks of COVID when it felt like everything stopped. My team at Adapt Productivity were faced with every bit of work booked in for the year ahead cancelling. None of us knew what was going to happen. The streets were empty, our offices silent, and our heads were trying to calculate how much worse things could get. They got much worse, but then they started to get better.

Many organisations put in plans to help their teams to work from home. We all got used to Zoom meetings, and then MS Teams meetings. Zoom trivia was all the rage on a Friday night until we all got sick of that. Slowly but surely work started to get back to some sort of normal, albeit a remote normal. During this period my team and I were very fortunate. We spent three months adapting our programs for online delivery, and our clients started to book work again. Productivity training was high on the list of priorities for many organisations, as people needed to get their heads around being productive from home and needed to learn how to harness the power of their productivity tools like MS Outlook and OneNote, as these tools had now become the umbilical cords between each member of the team.

We had so many learnings during this period and worked to incorporate these learnings and the new strategies we developed into our training programs. I want to share these with you now, as I believe you will benefit from a productivity system that has been forged by the necessity of our time.

And now we move into a new phase, where workers are coming back into the office again. But not all of them or 100% of the time. We are moving to another 'new normal'; the hybrid workplace. We cannot ignore the positives we all felt when working from home. More flexibility, less travel time, less distraction, more time to really focus. Most of us missed catching up with our colleagues and collaborating face-to-face, but we didn't want to lose these benefits and go back to our old way of working. So many businesses are trialling hybrid workplaces, where workers can work from the office or home. There are many models of what this looks like, and it will take another couple of years for the best models to rise to the top of this evolutionary tree, but we will move forward into this new way of working, make no mistake.

But we need to be productive now, whether we are in the office, at home, onsite or online. So, this version of *Smart Work* will take all of the strategies that still work so well in this new environment, and complement them with new strategies that have evolved in the face of the productivity issues created by our changing circumstances.

In the preface to the original *Smart Work* I talked about the fact that my company name, Adapt, was also my core aim in life. I help people to adapt in an ever-changing workplace. This is just another opportunity for all of us to adapt and evolve. My wish for you is that *Smart Work* helps to bring you a sense of control over your work, a sense of balance in your life, and a sense of satisfaction and achievement in your work.

Read this book from cover to cover if you are interested in a comprehensive approach to personal productivity using technology. Or dip in and grab an idea or strategy that you can implement straight away. But know this: if you do not adapt, you will be left behind, drowning in unprocessed emails, overwhelmed by your workload and feeling like you are getting nowhere in this brave new world.

It is time for smart work.

Introduction

The workplace has changed. How we work has changed. The pace of business has changed. How we communicate has changed, and the tools we are using to organise ourselves have changed. It stands to reason that we need to adapt our work practices to deal with these changes.

I wrote these words in 2016. Little did I know things would change even more. I should not be surprised, as it now seems obvious that every few years there will be major issues, or major breakthroughs, that shift how we work. The trick is to be adaptable and to embrace the positives of these changes, while at the same time developing new strategies to overcome the new workplace issues we face.

Productivity in the 21st century

From a productivity standpoint, our workplaces have seen massive changes over the past 50 years. Since the 1970s, we have moved from a traditional workplace to a digital workplace, and now to a hybrid workplace. We are no longer chained to desks and cubicles, or even tied to working in an open plan workspace in the office. Many of us are free to work from the office or from home, and can split our week into time spent working from both locations.

Over the years, the tools we use to organise our work have shifted from paper diaries to personal desktop organisers to sophisticated group scheduling systems. We have progressively moved from a paper-driven workplace to an electronic workplace with a computer on every desk and handheld devices to help us stay organised. Over the last few years, most knowledge workers have been furnished with laptops to enable remote working, and have access to all of their data and work information in the Cloud.

The challenges we face to stay productive have also changed. Many of us are now working in a global workplace, with colleagues and clients located all over the world. Even though hybrid working has meant that many of us have reclaimed travel time back into our day, we are working longer hours to keep up, and may be experiencing the dissolving of boundaries between our work and home life.

The workspace too has changed, from individual offices and cubicles to open plan for all and *activity-based working* where we don't even have our own desk. When working from home, some are lucky to have good workspaces set up for remote working, but many are faced with setting up in the bedroom or on the dining table to work. Not ideal.

Those of us that have experienced working remotely or working in a hybrid situation will have felt the disconnection that comes with working in a team that is geographically dispersed. Managers are challenged with staying close to their team, creating alignment and building the culture. Workers are challenged with the increase in the volume of emails, chat and meetings as everyone tries to stay connected. And everyone struggles with the fact that you can't just move things forward with a quick chat with your colleague across the desk, or in the corridor.

Massive changes to how we work and stay organised have occurred — some good, some not so good, but all very different from what we have been used to.

There are a range of issues that make it challenging for the modern worker to stay productive.

Too much to do, too little time

Today we have way more to do than we have time in which to do it. Most organisations expect management and staff to get more done with fewer resources. They are downsizing their workforces, but not downsizing the work! Add to this the number of meetings we are expected to attend, and the volume of emails we have to wade through, and it seems hard to imagine how we will get it all done.

Of course, many people are throwing the only weapon they feel they have available at the problem — more time. We are working longer hours to cope with the increased workload. Many senior managers I work with are in meetings between 9 am and 5 pm, then catch up on emails and other tasks between 5 pm and 9 pm. We know that this is not the solution! Working from home has fed into this problem, as people seem more ready to get the laptop out after dinner to catch up. Even though working from home gives us the ability to keep an eye on the kids or throw on a wash during our workday, working extended hours cannot be good for our wellbeing in the long run.

Information overload

As the volume of information we receive each day continues to grow, the pressure is becoming overwhelming. It is not unusual for me to work with managers who receive 300-plus emails per day. This is crazy! We do not need 300, or even 100 emails a day to do our jobs effectively. I would argue that these emails are actually *stopping* us from doing our jobs effectively. But that sense of overwhelm is definitely being felt at all levels in organisations.

Add to that the introduction of Instant Messaging (IM) and tools like MS Teams, and we are being constantly bombarded by requests, interruptions, messages and distractions. We need a solution, fast.

An increase in urgency

When is everything needed? Now! ASAP! Yesterday! Five minutes ago! We are under great pressure to deliver everything instantly, and this constant urgency is affecting the quality of our work. It is causing reactivity in the workplace that is increasing stress levels, increasing working hours, and decreasing the quality of our thinking and outputs.

This reactivity has come to be accepted as the norm in many organisations. In fact, this way of work was so alarming to me that I wrote a book about it in 2018. 'Urgent' is the new 'important' in many organisations.

'But that's just the way it is around here', they say. It's just how it is in global finance, the legal sector, the insurance industry, even in the consulting industry. Well, I don't agree. I do not accept that it has to be that way. I believe that to a large degree this urgency has been driven by the 'instant' nature of electronic communication. Certainly we need to ensure that we all work together with a *sense of urgency* to get things done. But have we gone too far with this, creating instead *senseless urgency*?

Sometimes I imagine myself as a superhero, flying in to save the day in my clients' offices. If I was, I would have to have a nemesis, an arch-enemy. The enemy I have sworn to banish from as many organisations as I can get to is *unnecessary urgency*.

I see workers battle with urgency every day. And they are losing. They are becoming resigned to the fact that this is 'just the way it is around here'.

A lack of balance

Work/life balance is a hot topic in many organisations, along with wellbeing, stress and mental health. Many leaders now recognise that productivity needs to be sustainable, and if their people are constantly under pressure, they will burn out. Yet, many people I work with have no sense of balance. To achieve work/life balance, you need to first achieve work/work balance, and most people's work is far from balanced. We give too much of our core working hours to meetings, and therefore have no balance between time spent meeting with others and time protected for other important priorities. We work too reactively, so have no balance between the urgent issues that demand our attention and time spent working proactively on other work. And we focus too much on distractions like emails, rather than ensuring our work is driven by the objectives we are trying to achieve.

Still using outdated tools and strategies to organise our work

Finally, and for me this is the most crucial issue, we are not leveraging the technology at our fingertips enough — tools like Microsoft Outlook or Google Calendar™ (or whichever email and calendar platform your organisation uses), and the smartphones and tablets that can sync with our computer-based tools. We use these tools every day, but in my experience most of us are not really harnessing their power. In fact, I would suggest that the average worker probably uses about 20 per cent of the functionality of a tool like Outlook. And yet this is the first thing they turn on every day to check their email. We learn the basics — how to send an email, how to schedule a meeting. But few of us go on to utilise these powerful tools in a holistic way to organise our time, priorities and information.

Instead, we are grappling with modern productivity issues using old-fashioned tools and strategies. Paper lists, sticky notes and piles of paper — none of these answer the challenges of managing our work in the modern workplace. We need to get smart about leveraging our technology.

So what is the solution?

Three key productivity killers thread their way through all of the issues raised above: busyness, urgency and distraction. My favourite book since childhood is *The Lord of the Rings*. I must have read it twenty times over. When I think of these three productivity killers, I think of the black riders, or Nazgul, in the book. Frodo and his fellowship are constantly harried by these demons, and need to be brave and strong in the face of their terror.

We also need to be strong in the face of busyness, urgency and distraction. We need good systems to fight these productivity demons. We need to be disciplined and build habits that serve us and keep us focused on the right work to achieve the outcomes we need to in our role. And we need to harness the power of our technology to give ourselves the edge in what is often an unfair fight.

And all of this is even more important if we are working in a hybrid or remote workplace, where we are less connected to our team and our team culture.

Of course, productivity is not just a personal issue. It can be worked on at the individual level, at the team level or at the organisational level. But it always starts with the individual — how we behave, what we choose to focus on, what we allow to drive our day.

And productivity is not just about getting more done. It is about getting more of the right things done in a balanced and sustainable way.

This book is designed to help you to work more productively using the *Smart Work system* (illustrated in figure A, overleaf) that I have developed over the past 20 years while working with corporate clients. It sets out the steps and strategies to help you take control of how you organise and keep track of your incoming work (inputs), what you spend your time on each working day (actions) and what you achieve (outcomes).

The Smart Work system at a glance

Increasing your productivity is not just a case of implementing a few tips and tricks, and it's not solely about email management or how you organise your priorities. True productivity in the 21st century workplace requires a more sophisticated approach. That does not mean it has to be complex, though. All of the productivity strategies in *Smart Work* can be implemented to increase your productivity in a simple and practical way.

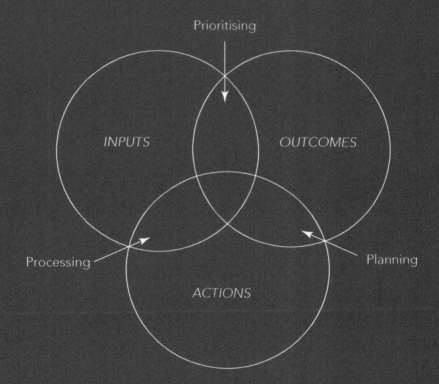

Figure A: integrated productivity system

Centralise your actions

As our work becomes more complex, we need a system to manage what we need to do and when we need to do it. Centralisation is the key. To manage our *actions*, commitments and priorities effectively, we need to have everything centralised in one organising tool.

Having everything in one place gives you focus, clarity and a better ability to prioritise. The electronic calendar has become the default tool for managing meetings and appointments, and has been embraced widely in the corporate workplace. The calendar centralises all of your meetings in one place, and it works pretty well most of the time. But you also have many, many tasks and priorities to juggle outside of meetings. This is where systems become decentralised, with work buried in separate 'piles'. This is neither efficient nor effective.

The case for using electronic calendars as your main meeting scheduling tool is obvious to most. Meetings happen in collaboration with others. Our schedules are complex, and using a system that allows us to clearly check everyone's availability and lock in mutually convenient meeting times seems only logical.

The case for using an electronic task list is not so clear to many, so fewer have made the leap to ditch their paper lists in favour of digital tools. For me, it all boils down to one simple but compelling function. With the click of a button emails can be converted into tasks and scheduled as prioritised actions in tools like Outlook! Just as you benefit from the efficiency of meeting invitations that are scheduled at the agreed time once accepted, your productivity will be increased once you begin to schedule emails as tasks to be prioritised and completed at the appropriate time.

So you need one tool to manage your meetings and one tool to manage your tasks. Just taking that first step towards centralisation will increase your focus and effectiveness. And if you create a system that combines both your meetings and your priorities in one view, it is very likely that your sense of control and productivity will undergo a massive increase, as you start to manage all of your activities from one platform.

Organise your inputs

Once you have set up a centralised system for managing your actions, you need to look at what feeds this system. How does work arrive on your desk (or in your inbox), and how do you make good decisions about what work should get your time and attention? These *inputs* are the second element that needs to be considered in your integrated productivity system.

Many of us receive hundreds of inputs every day in the form of emails, phone calls, voicemails, instant messages, physical interruptions, meeting actions and thoughts. Much of this is just noise and does not deserve much of our time and attention, but some of it is important and does need action. Should we do it now or later, though? We need to avoid reacting instantly to every incoming email, but at the same time, we don't want this work just to pile up until it overwhelms us.

The key to managing your inputs effectively is to take a proactive approach to processing incoming work and to create a connection between your inputs system and your actions system. New inputs that need your attention should be either dealt with immediately or recorded in your action management system, depending on their urgency. Using your inbox as an action system for emails does not work, as you just end up with a pile of 'action emails' buried in a pile of 'non-action emails', with no sense of their respective priority or timing.

Your inbox has one purpose, and that is to receive emails. Just like the letterbox outside your house, it should be emptied regularly and the mail dealt with appropriately. Of course, on any given day you will receive way more emails than letters, and you need strategies to reduce the noise so you only have to deal with relevant messages. You also need an efficient filing system in place so you can file things quickly and easily — and find them again just as quickly and easily.

Your ability to manage the flow of incoming work, whether it is email or any other form of input, is critical to your productivity. If you do not control your inbox, it will control you. Email is not the main reason you have a job. You could contribute so much more than that, if you only had the time. We need to make the time by being clever and harnessing the power of technology.

Realise your outcomes

If efficiency was your only productivity goal, then processing your inputs and managing your actions would achieve it. But to be truly productive, you also need to work effectively. To work effectively you need to look at one more core element in the system — your *outcomes*. To ensure you are doing the right work, you need clarity of purpose. What are you trying to achieve? What are your goals and objectives? Where do you want to end up? You need to look beyond simply reacting to everyone else's needs and proactively schedule into your system the right actions that will help you to achieve the right results.

To do this you first need to clarify what you are trying to achieve and get some perspective on what is really important in your role. Your goals and objectives are often linked to team, departmental, divisional and organisational goals and objectives. In most organisations, much time and effort goes into creating performance plans that align and cascade to ensure everyone is pulling in the same direction. But does this really drive your activity on an individual level, and on a day-to-day basis? Not often enough, I fear. There is frequently a disconnect between what you are trying to achieve and what you are actually spending your time on.

Taking time out to plan and prioritise is crucial to creating both clarity of purpose and a connection between your outcomes and your actions. Creating regular spaces where you stop *doing* and think about the bigger picture is the real key to working effectively.

The practices that drive productivity

So your actions, inputs and outcomes come together in an integrated system for working productively. Yet systems only organise information. You still need to do the work, and you need to feed and maintain the system constantly to ensure it keeps you organised and moving forward. There are three key practices that maintain and sustain the integrated productivity system. They will keep you on track, even when you are at your busiest, and will allow you to be productive without even having to think about it — they will, in other words, shape 'the way you work'.

In his book *The Power of Habit*, Charles Duhigg discusses 'keystone habits'. These habits, once formed, increase the chances of other habits forming successfully. Processing, planning and prioritising are the keystone habits for maintaining the integrated productivity system.

1. **Processing.** Processing connects your actions and your inputs. It is the practice of proactively reviewing your incoming information and making decisions about what needs to happen to every input. Processing your inbox(es) down to zero once a week is one of the most effective strategies for working productively and focusing on the important work that deserves your precious time. Processing ensures that you are on top of the flow of incoming work but not dominated by it.

2. **Planning.** Monthly, weekly and daily planning rituals create the connection between your outcomes (what you want to achieve) and your actions (what you will do). Each planning routine has a particular intent. Monthly planning gives you perspective; weekly planning gets you organised; and daily planning gets you focused for the day ahead. Planning ensures you are doing the right work at the right time — that you are being proactively productive.

3. **Prioritising.** Processing and planning both involve prioritisation. But as a practice, prioritising should stand alone. Prioritising helps you to manage the opportunity cost of spending your time unproductively, and sits at the heart of effectiveness. If you have more to do than you have time available (and who doesn't), prioritisation helps you to consider all the things you could invest your time in, and choose the right actions. Prioritising therefore creates a connection between outcomes and inputs.

In the pages that follow, I unpack and explore the integrated productivity system in depth, suggesting simple, practical ways you can incorporate it into your day-to-day work and better leverage the technology already at your fingertips. So if this sounds like an approach that could revolutionise your work life, let's get stuck in and get productive!

The Smart Work roadmap — nine productivity skills

This section is designed to provide an overview map for the book. The principles outlined in figure B represent the key areas you need to focus on to clarify, organise and protect your time, priorities and commitments. Use this section to navigate to topics of interest or to zoom out to see how the productivity practices fit together.

So we have looked at how Actions, Inputs and Outcomes work together in an integrated way. Now let's unbundle the three key principles that sit under each of these areas of our productivity.

By the way, I am fully aware that to many it would seem to make more sense to look at our inputs first, then our actions and then our outcomes. This is a sensible progression. But there is good reason why I have chosen the sequence I have. My experience is that we need to set up a foundation to manage our actions, before we can effectively manage either inputs or outcomes. If we do not have a way to action work in a timely way, it is impossible to get on top of our incoming work. And getting traction with our outcomes relies heavily on having a good action management system.

So the nine chapters of the book correspond to the nine productivity skills of the Smart Work roadmap. Here's how the chapters break down.

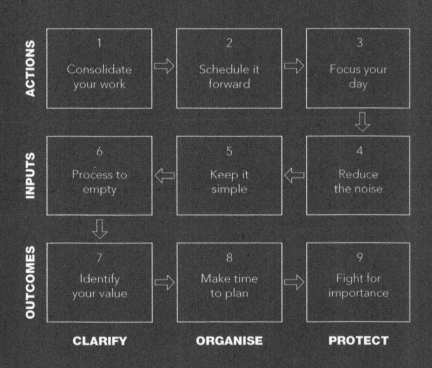

Figure B: the Smart Work roadmap

Actions

1. **Consolidate your work.** The starting point for your new productivity system is to clarify everything that currently needs your time and attention. This chapter will help you to achieve clarity through centralising all of your actions into one electronic organising tool.

2. **Schedule it forward.** To manage your actions in a proactive way, you need to link the resource of time to the things you need to do. This can be achieved by scheduling both meetings and tasks in a proactive scheduling system that will allow you to focus on the right work at the right time, as outlined in this chapter.

3. **Focus your day.** Without a plan, your day can easily be hijacked by everyone else's crises. With a plan, you can begin to control how your day plays out, and therefore what you actually get done. This chapter outlines a range of strategies to help you to get focused and to protect your focus from the distractions in your busy workplace.

Inputs

4. **Reduce the noise.** The volume of non-essential information that vies for our attention is constantly increasing. This noise prevents us from focusing on more important work. It is crucial that we protect ourselves from noise as much as possible. This chapter looks at a number of strategies you can use to control the noise levels.

5. **Keep it simple.** One reason many people do not have control of their inbox is that their filing system is too complicated. This chapter explores strategies for

managing and filing emails quickly, and finding them again quickly.

6. **Process to empty.** Most people see their inbox as a never-ending list of work tasks. They use it to manage their email priorities — and end up feeling stressed, out of control and demotivated. It doesn't have to be like that. This chapter focuses on the strategies needed to get your inbox to empty on a regular basis. This puts you in control of your inbox, and provides clarity as you work out what needs your attention and what does not.

Outcomes

7. **Identify your value.** Many of us have performance plans, key result areas, key performance indicators and objectives coming out of our ears. But it can be hard to stay focused on the right work to achieve these outcomes. This chapter looks at how you can gain clarity in your role by looking at the big picture and working out the activities that will really make a difference.

8. **Make time to plan.** Many teams undertake a range of quarterly or monthly team planning exercises, yet few of us stop to personally plan our time and effort. We are usually too busy to stop and take time out to plan. Chapter 8 looks at three levels of personal planning that will help you to get organised and focused on the right work.

9. **Fight for importance.** It doesn't matter how much effort we put into planning and organising our priorities, other people will have different ideas. They

will feel that their work is more important or more urgent than ours. And they will ramp up the pressure to get what they need, now! We need to dial down this urgency and protect our priorities by fighting for what we believe to be important. This final chapter looks at strategies that can reduce the focus on urgency and protect some of your time for the truly important work that will actually make a significant difference.

Processing, planning and prioritising

As already noted, the three core practices that you should build habits around, and that will drive your productivity behaviours, are processing, planning and prioritising. At the end of each part we will explore one of these practices in detail in a key practice feature.

A note on technology

Now we have examined the core areas we need to focus on to work productively in the modern workplace, we should take a look at the tools available to us when implementing these principles, practices and skills.

The first step to working productively in the modern workplace is to meet the productivity challenges we face with the appropriate tools — 21st century tools. As the volume and complexity of our work increases, we need to leverage technology to help us deal with this complexity. Relying on our overtaxed brains to remember everything is no longer a viable option. Paper tools such as lists and calendars cease to be relevant when so much of our work is driven by email.

You need more sophisticated tools to manage the sheer volume of emails and the complexity of your busy days. The good news is you have these tools at your fingertips already — you just might not be leveraging them enough or using them in an integrated way. In fact, you may be applying a 20th century methodology to a 21st century tool!

There are a plethora of devices, apps and software programs available to help people to work more productively, although most corporate environments use a few standard productivity tools across the organisation. These can be broadly split into personal productivity tools, team productivity tools and mobile productivity tools.

Personal productivity tools

Every organisation, big or small, uses some form of personal productivity software to manage emails and schedules. In my experience, most medium to large organisations use MS Outlook as their core email client. Some use Lotus Notes (fewer and fewer), and a number have switched to Gmail™ and Google Calendar over the past few years. Microsoft has been the traditional big player in this space, with Outlook leading the race in terms of the number of organisations using it. While all of the principles that I discuss in this book can be applied to any electronic tool, I will focus mainly on Outlook. For this reason, however, I will endeavour to discuss how techniques can be applied to Lotus Notes or Gmail if different from Outlook. While I may refer only to Outlook at times, take it that I am talking about all three platforms.

MS Outlook

So Outlook is installed on your desktop or laptop. You use it every day to manage your email. But how else do you use

Outlook? What other parts of Outlook do you leverage to boost your productivity? What functions do you regularly use to stay on top of your workflow? Maybe not as many as you could or should.

In Part I we will look at how tools such as Outlook were designed to be used as a one-stop shop to manage all your activities. With most of your work driven by email these days, it made sense for Microsoft to design workload management functions around the inbox. So Outlook has a *calendar* and a *task* list, both designed to manage your actions. It also contains a *contacts* folder, a *notes* folder and, of course, *filing* folders, designed to help you to keep and retain information (see figure C). We will examine how to make all of these functions work together as one cohesive system for managing your workflow. If you get this right, you can discard many of the paper tools that you have relied upon for so many years but that no longer serve their purpose in the email environment.

OneNote

A note-taking program that has long been a part of the Microsoft Office suite, OneNote allows you to capture notes, agendas and actions in a range of notebooks, which can be shared with others in the team. It links to Outlook, so meeting details can easily be linked to the notes, and meeting actions can be scheduled straight into your task list in Outlook. This is a very under-utilised tool, which is a pity, as it is such a powerful complement to MS Outlook. They work together to help you to manage your time (Outlook) and information (OneNote).

Evernote®

Similar to OneNote, Evernote is a popular program that works across your devices and is great for managing meeting notes, as well as capturing ideas and organising information. Evernote

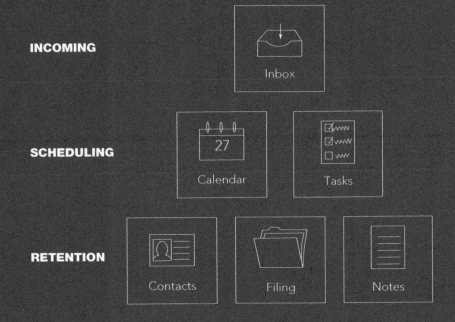

INCOMING — Inbox

SCHEDULING — Calendar — Tasks

RETENTION — Contacts — Filing — Notes

Figure C: workload management in Outlook

is often used in organisations that are less reliant on Microsoft Office.

Team productivity tools

As this book is focused primarily on personal productivity, I won't spend a lot of time on the following tools. But they are a part of the mix and rate a mention, as they can cause problems when managing our personal productivity if not considered and managed well.

- **MS Teams.** This is a collaboration platform that has been around for a while, but has only really gained traction as a result of COVID and the shift to remote working. It has fast become a core tool for many teams who are working collaboratively across multiple locations. It has the ability to manage information and discussions around projects and other collaborative work, as well as virtual meetings and a chat function.

- **MS Planner.** Most individuals and teams don't need complicated tools like Microsoft Project to plan the more complex work they are responsible for. But they do sometimes need tools to help visualise the work and to collaborate with others in a smart way. Planner is a visual project board that allows you to make all of the work in a project visible for you and your team. It can organise the project actions in a highly visual way, and allow you to keep track of who is doing what and the progress of each activity. I believe that many teams should use this tool more than they do because when you make work visible across the team, it becomes more manageable.

- **Other cloud project-planning tools.** There are now many other online project tools, such as Asana, Trello and Jira, that can help you and your team to plan and manage projects. These are great for organisations that are not using Office 365. But if you are, I would highly recommend that you stick to Planner as it lives within the Office ecosystem, and it connects better with tools like Outlook, MS Teams and OneNote.

Mobile productivity tools

What if you are not at your desk? Some form of paper (a notepad, a printout of your schedule or printed emails) may be needed to stay organised on the run. But with the right mobile technology you can dispense with most of these as well. There is a wide range of tablet PCs, smartphones and handheld devices available to help you to stay organised on the run. Again, though, you may not be taking advantage of these tools and their capabilities, beyond glancing at emails when in meetings.

Many organisations have deployed smartphones and tablets for certain roles or levels of management, or have introduced a BYO policy for devices. At the time of writing, Apple iOS and Android seem to be most popular, with Windows Mobile close behind. For simplicity, I will refer to Apple iOS devices, as these are the most prevalent, but all concepts can usually be applied to most mobile devices.

I believe the key to harnessing your mobile technology to help you stay productive on the run is to ensure that your device synchronises with all of the core elements in your desktop tool. Ideally your email, calendar, tasks, contacts and notes should sync across to your device and back again. This means you can stay organised anywhere, without duplication. You can process emails on the run and need touch them only once. You can schedule or reschedule meetings, as well as check your meeting commitments for the day ahead. You can capture tasks in your centralised list when away from your desk and take advantage of any spare moments in your day to knock a couple of items off the list. And you can access all your contact details and miscellaneous notes. What a perfect system!

Other tools mentioned above also have mobile equivalents. I use OneNote on my phone and iPad every day, and it syncs perfectly to OneNote on my desktop. MS Teams can be accessed through a mobile app, as can MS Planner for updating projects on the run.

The technology is already here. You just need to think about how you can best take advantage of it.

So you have a range of electronic tools at your disposal. But to really leverage their power, you need to use them in a synchronised way. Recently a participant in one of my workshops made a really good point about his use of technology. He considered himself a reasonably effective user of technology and had definitely made the shift from paper tools to digital technology. He used Outlook to manage his emails, schedule and priorities. He used OneNote for capturing meeting notes and a number of apps on his iPhone to manage task lists on the run.

His insight was about *how* he used these tools. While he used them all every day, he used each one in isolation. He was not coordinating how he managed the information across these platforms. This meant he had a task list in Outlook but other task lists in an app on his phone, and yet more task lists in OneNote.

Using electronic tools in isolation will definitely be more effective than using paper, but as I will demonstrate throughout this book, true leverage comes from using these tools in a coordinated way.

Finally, a note on tech tips and hybrid hacks: As so much of this book focuses on working smarter with your technology, it makes sense to include some highly practical technology tips in each chapter. Every chapter finishes with a tech tips section that outlines some relevant technology strategies to help you to implement the concepts discussed in that chapter.

And, in the process of rewriting *Smart Work* for today's (and tomorrow's) workplace, I think it would make sense to talk about a range of strategies to help you to manage your actions, inputs and outcomes when working in a hybrid or remote context. You will also find a 'Hybrid Help' section at the end of each of the three main parts of the book. In these sections I will discuss some of the productivity issues that are particular to hybrid working, and the strategies you could employ to overcome them.

So, on to the first section — Actions. Let's build a foundation for our productivity system that will help us to manage our activities in an efficient, effective and proactive way.

PART I
Centralise Your Actions

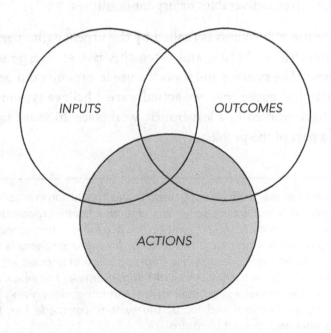

Busyness is a mindset. Or to paraphrase Peter Cook, author of *The New Rules of Management*, busyness is an emotional response to our schedule. We feel busy when our schedule or task list is full. When someone asks us how we are we respond instinctively: 'Busy'.

But what does this really mean? Are we not always busy with something? Yes, of course we will have pressure points when major deadlines loom, or when a project is in full swing, but these particularly busy times seem to have become the norm. There are fewer and fewer gaps between our busy periods, which for many have joined up into one never-ending busy period. The only thing that changes is the content of this week's crises, deliverables or urgent deadlines.

This sense of busyness is fuelled by the urgency that pervades our modern workplace, and often this is a self-perpetuating problem. The systems and tools we use to organise our actions make us feel busier than we actually are. I believe systems that may have worked in a less frantic workplace 20 years ago are now a part of the problem.

A client I worked with recently came to this conclusion in a training session. A typically busy senior manager in a health organisation, he was desperate for help to get on top of a full meeting schedule and an overflowing inbox. His strategy for managing emails was simply to let them pile up while flagging any that needed action. Unfortunately he then had lots of flagged emails. His inbox was his system for managing email inputs, but rather than giving him a feeling of control and focus, the system just made him feel overwhelmed and out of control.

Interestingly, of the fifty-odd items in his inbox that he had flagged for action, a large number turned out to be low priority industry-related reading. These articles and newsletters were useful reading, but none were critical to his day-to-day role. Maybe six emails were priorities that he needed to deal with in the next few days.

So this manager was feeling busy because of the growing list of flagged messages in his inbox, yet the reality was that most of it was non-critical work. While the flags helped to identify emails that still needed attention, his problem was that his system for managing actions set everything at the same level of priority and urgency in his mind, which created a distorted sense of how busy he really was. By batching together his reading emails, and prioritising and scheduling the real actions, he began to experience a sense of control and clarity that he had not felt in a long while.

Was he busy? Yes. Had he been feeling busier than he should have because of an ineffective management system? Definitely.

This part of the book focuses on how to manage your actions in a systematic way. It shows you what you need to do and when you need to do it.

The first step is to collect all the things that need your time and attention and put them in one place. As chapter 1 will show, consolidating all your actions in this way will bring clarity. In chapter 2 we will look at a powerful strategy for proactively organising your priorities in a forward schedule. This will ensure you do the right work at the right time. In chapter 3 we will look at ways you can protect your time and create increased focus using a daily plan. Your time is your most precious resource; it is critical that you manage your activities within the context of this resource.

The concepts explored in this section all build towards setting up a centralised system for managing your meetings and your tasks. I would strongly suggest that this central system should be electronic—either Outlook or whatever calendar and email tool you are currently using. Not only does this make managing your work more efficient, but it makes sense as you have probably already committed to using this system for all of your meetings.

CHAPTER 1
Consolidate your work

Our work day is made up of two types of actions—meetings and tasks (see figure 1.1). Whatever your industry or role, to work effectively you need to manage both of these types of work. I believe we face a fundamental challenge in managing these two activities, as they are very different, and require different strategies to organise them well.

Meetings vs tasks

Meetings are what we call *fixed work*—that is, they are fixed in time: they need to happen at a specific time, and they have fixed start and (usually) finish times. This is mainly because other people are involved in meetings, so a time and location must be agreed to. Some roles are driven by meetings, while other roles may entail just a couple of meetings each week.

When you are not in meetings, you are probably doing tasks. Sending emails, writing reports and preparing for presentations

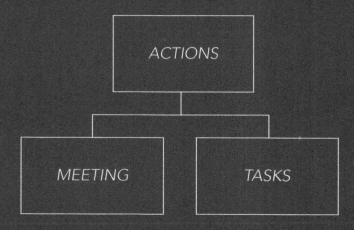

Figure 1.1: meetings and tasks

are examples of tasks. Tasks may be date-specific without being time-specific. Unlike fixed meetings, tasks usually need to be done *by* a certain time, rather than *at* a certain time. Because of this they have a level of discretion attached to them. It is up to you when you do them. I call these actions *flexible*. You might commit to calling someone tomorrow without specifying what time you will call. This makes it a task rather than a meeting. I believe what is needed more than anything to manage tasks effectively is flexibility. You need to be able to move things around, reschedule, re-prioritise and fit things into the cracks between other commitments.

Having worked with thousands of people over the past two decades, I have noticed some common behaviours around how most people manage their meetings and tasks. These behaviours can hinder your efforts to manage your work in a focused and proactive way:

- Meetings are scheduled in one central calendar while tasks are often captured in lots of places.

- Most of us can get to a meeting on time but often seem to leave tasks until the last minute.

- Meetings are usually managed using technology; tasks are too often managed using paper-based tools or our memory.

- Meetings are highly public while tasks may be private until they are due, or overdue.

These have profound implications for our productivity. The fact that we have embraced technology to manage our meeting workload but are, for the most part, still using paper tools to manage our task priorities has led to an imbalance in how we manage our time. In effect, we only really plan the use of this resource (time) when we schedule meetings, which may account for just half of our workload. Using task management tools that separate our task workload from our meeting workload and do not manage tasks within the context of time can lead to many productivity problems.

So what happened? Why did we shift so readily to electronic calendars but not to electronic task lists?

Meeting tools — the shift from paper to electronic

Meetings are a highly public type of work: if we forget a meeting it is visible to all involved. We need to remember when and where our meetings are happening, so in most cases we have adopted whatever group calendar tool is in place in our organisation. While there could be design improvements to all of these systems, in general they allow us to manage our meeting workload easily and effectively.

So what do we need a calendar to do for us to ensure we turn up to the right meeting at the right time? We need to be able to schedule our meetings for a specific day and a specific time. We need to block out our time between the start and the finish of the meeting so we don't double book, and we need to be able to see at a glance what we have scheduled for our day or week. In the 20th century workplace a paper diary did all of these things perfectly well, yet when electronic scheduling systems such as Outlook arrived, in most cases there was a rapid and enthusiastic adoption of the new technology. Today most medium to large organisations in which people use computers and have access to email also use an electronic calendar.

These electronic scheduling systems brought additional benefits to the table for an increasingly busy workforce. They increased efficiency, as we no longer had to rewrite our diary entries when things changed—we could just move them with the click of a button. They brought greater visibility, as we could now zoom in and out of our schedule, from day to month view. But the greatest benefit was increased collaboration, as we could now send meeting invites that made it easier to coordinate a mutually convenient time to meet with groups of people, possibly in different locations. We could now check other people's availability and choose appropriate times to meet with them. Managers could give their executive assistants access to their calendar, which meant visibility for both and reduced duplication, error and confusion.

So the electronic calendar provided a more efficient, flexible and trustworthy system for managing meetings. But this technology has not been picked up with the same enthusiasm to manage the other half of our work—our tasks and priorities. Let's have a look at how most workers tend to manage these.

Task tools—stuck in the 20th century

The flexible nature of tasks makes them a much more complex beast to manage. Tasks generally don't have to be done at specific times, so their timely completion is much more at the mercy of our willpower and discipline. And tasks are a more private type of work. The deadlines we need to meet in our roles are public, and it becomes a problem if we don't meet the due date, but *when* we do our work is our own affair. Most people don't care when we do it, as long as it is done by the deadline!

This has led to task systems that focus on the deadline, with no thought to the start date or when we are actually going to put time aside to do the work. So we tend to pile work up in all sorts of places depending on how the work arrived, whether in our inbox, our meeting notebook or our head. We might write a to-do list, but this often just specifies due dates, not when we are going to do the work. These disparate 'piles' can lead to the following problems:

- You don't have a central view of everything you need to do.

- You don't plan the activities within the context of your most precious resource — time.

- Your meeting and task workloads become unbalanced.

- You don't prioritise your work as effectively as you should.

- You often end up working reactively rather than proactively.

There are two issues that most concern me with these ineffective task systems. Firstly, there is no sense of priority with a pile. What is your most important next task — the email in your inbox, the paperwork on your desk, the call to return flagged on the sticky note on your computer screen, or the next task on your to-do list?

Secondly, there is no real commitment to when you are going to do the work. Without at least a rough date for when you will complete, or at least start, the task, there is a real risk that the work will get left in the pile until it becomes urgent.

To work effectively in the modern workplace you need to set up a system to manage your actions that takes advantage of your electronic tools, a system that has the following four essential characteristics.

Firstly, you need *flexibility*. Your meeting workload is relatively fixed, but your task workload is flexible by nature. You need to be able to move things around and make changes as your priorities change, and to do this quickly and without friction. You also need *visibility*. If your priorities are not visible to you when you need to see them, there is a risk that you will forget them and will end up leaving things until the last minute. To be truly focused on your most important work, you also need a sense of your *priorities*. And lastly, you need a system that encourages *proactivity*. You should manage your time and attention proactively, and make sure you are doing the right work at the right time.

The following approach will help you to adopt an effective way of managing your actions.

Centralise absolutely every action

Centralise all of your actions in one place.

Your work reaches you in many different ways. You have externally driven work that comes in the form of emails, physical interruptions and meeting actions. This work can be reactive and is often operational in nature. You also have internally driven work that you should do to progress your objectives and projects. Whatever way the work arrives, centralising all of it in one place will help you to manage it effectively.

In my experience, most people don't have their tasks centralised. They are usually captured in a range of places. Which of the following do you use to keep track of all the things you need to do?

- Inbox

- To-do list

- Meeting notes

- Paper piles on your desk

- Sticky notes

- Your head

- Voicemail

- OneNote lists

- Project plans

Because your work arrives through different channels, you can fall into the trap of automatically managing the action in the place that it arrived. For example, you may leave emails in your inbox until you have dealt with them or leave reports on your desk until they are needed. You try to remember things to do, until they become urgent or overdue. In other words, by default, you are organising your work based on how it arrives rather than how important it is or when it needs to be done.

Organising all email actions together, or all paper-driven actions together, does not help you to get the right work done at the right time. And it does not help you to prioritise what is most important. Your work will just build up in piles and may become urgent before you finally get to it. The fact that these piles are not integrated means that you may lose sight of some of the tasks and reduce your ability to prioritise your work.

One of the first steps to regaining control is to centralise all of your tasks in one organising tool. When your actions are buried in separate piles, organising and consolidating them can seem daunting or even overwhelming. But it is really quite a simple process and for most people should not take more than a couple of hours. The benefit will be that you will have much more clarity about what needs your time and attention.

Your aim is to make everything you need to do visible in one central place. As I have said, your meetings are probably centralised in your calendar already, so that just leaves your tasks and priorities. Use the following process to get your task workload centralised.

Consider — Capture — Commit

Get everything centralised ASAP.

The next step is to capture all your tasks in one place. The best way to do this is to set aside the time to do a total scan of all actions and next steps that require your time and attention.

There are three phases to this total scan.

1. Consider

Identify all of the ways that your tasks will currently be listed. These could be places where the tasks are currently sitting, such as your inbox or your written to-do list, or they could be contexts, such as different roles or projects. Identifying these will help you to brainstorm a more complete list of actions.

Here are some questions to assist you in creating your list:

- What tasks are in my inbox?

- What is currently on my to-do list?

- Do I have any calls to make/return?

- Are there tasks in previous meeting notes that still need to be actioned?

- Is there paperwork on my desk reminding me to do something?

- What about those sticky notes on my computer screen?

- What else is stuck in my head?

- What are the next-step tasks related to my current projects?

- Do I need to prepare for any upcoming meetings?

- Are there personal things I need to do?

- What should I be doing within the context of my core roles?

2. Capture

Once you have considered your task locations, spend some time capturing absolutely every task you can see or think of that deserves your time and attention. This can be done using paper or electronically using a tool such as Excel or Word.

Don't stop to complete any of these actions (even though you may feel compelled to when you spot some of the more urgent ones). Just spend the time brainstorming, collecting and capturing.

3. Commit

Once you have created your exhaustive set of lists, you need to think about when you are going to allocate time to the action. This is an extremely important factor that will make the difference between inaction and traction. You need to commit to *when*. When are you going to allocate time to the action? Without this there is a risk that you will make the lists but not actually do anything. Your tasks need time commitment to get traction.

In the coming chapters we will be looking at the best way to schedule these actions. Some may end up as tasks in your centralised system; some may end up as time blocked out in your calendar; and some may end up being discussed in meetings or delegated to others.

We will also look at a proactive scheduling system that will help you to take what is probably a very large list (or several) and break it down into manageable and realistic pieces.

But first spend some time getting clarity by doing the Consider–Capture–Commit exercise. Do it low tech or do it high tech, just do it and get yourself set to really get organised.

Types of actions—hard to soft

Work out the best way to schedule the action.

Different actions need to be managed in different ways. Some of our activities, such as meetings, are fixed. They happen on a specific date at a specific time. At the other end of the continuum are tasks that you will need to do at some stage but you are not yet in a position to even think about when. We need different tools and strategies to manage these different types of activity and all of the activities in between. If you schedule a non-critical activity into your calendar, it just creates noise. If you put an upcoming meeting on a list somewhere, you will probably forget to go. You need the right tool for the job.

Figure 1.2 outlines five ways you could schedule an action in your calendar or task list. They range from very flexible undated lists, which have no scheduled dates attached to them, to fixed activities such as meetings, which are scheduled for a specific date, time and duration.

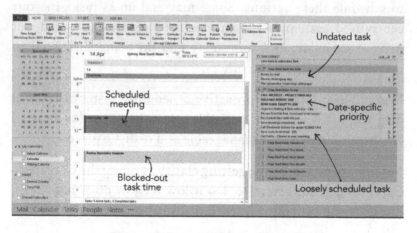

Figure 1.2: activities in Outlook

Undated task lists

Sometimes you may need to capture an action without actually committing to a time to do it. For example, you may need to capture an idea, a future action (beyond the short term), a project task or a discussion item for one of your team. These tasks need to be captured now, but will not be scheduled yet. The lists can be reviewed and the actions scheduled when the time is right. Further on in this chapter we will look at some different places that you can capture these actions, depending on their context.

Loosely scheduled tasks

Many of the things you need to do in the short to medium term should be loosely scheduled as tasks for a particular date over the next couple of weeks or months. For example, you might need to follow up with a client in the next few weeks, so you schedule the call for Monday week. You may or may not make the call on that day, but that is when you will start to consider that piece of work again. These tasks should be seen as 'nice to do' actions for the date they are scheduled and may need to be rescheduled if you do not get to them.

Date-specific priorities

There are some actions that must happen on a particular date but not necessarily at a specific time. If you make a commitment to call someone on Thursday, that is a date-specific action. These tasks should be scheduled for the appropriate day and highlighted in some way so they stand out as a critical priority for that day. In the old days we would highlight these tasks with an asterisk or a highlighter pen, or by making them an 'A' priority.

Blocked-out time

Some tasks need to be blocked out as events in your calendar. While this is overkill for most flexible activities, it works well for:

- tasks that must be done at a specific time

- complex work (anything that requires more than an hour of concentration)

- tasks you might otherwise procrastinate over

- other time usage, such as travel time and lunch time.

By blocking out time in your calendar you will be protecting your time in two ways. Firstly, it will be harder for other people to steal it away by inviting you to meetings at that time. Secondly, it will protect you from your own procrastination.

Meetings

A meeting is a fixed-time activity because other people are involved in the event. You need to lock in a date, time and duration and a location (which may be virtual). Your calendar is the obvious place to capture this information as it is purpose-built to manage specific timed events.

Understanding the best way to schedule an activity in your centralised action management system helps you to balance your work. Having a range of strategies at your disposal allows you to use the best tool for the job and creates a balance between fixed and flexible approaches.

Zoom in, zoom out

Zoom in and out of your schedule to execute and plan.

What is the right level of perspective needed to work effectively? I believe this depends on what you are doing, but broadly speaking we need to zoom out when we are planning and zoom in when we are executing our plans. If we stay at the same level all the time, we reduce our ability to work productively.

Writing this book required constant zooming in and out. I needed to zoom in to paragraph and sentence level when writing, but if I stayed locked in the detail for too long I would lose sight of the bigger picture. At regular intervals I needed to zoom out to the chapter and part levels to review progress and plan adjustments.

When managing actions, people often tend to stay locked into one level. They are either always zoomed out, looking at everything scheduled for the week, or they are zoomed in, focusing only on what is right in front of them. Optimal productivity requires flexibility, and zooming in and out provides the right perspective and level of detail at the right time. The trick is knowing which level is most appropriate.

When you are planning, zooming out of your schedule to view the week helps give you perspective. You see the whole picture, you get context and you can make better decisions because of this. When you are on a road trip and using Google Maps™, zooming out helps you to plan a route or orientate yourself on the map. You can get a better sense of where you are, where you are going and what might be the best way to get there. Once you have your route planned, you can zoom in to follow the turn-by-turn directions.

When you are doing your work, or executing your plan, zooming in helps you to focus. A day view in your calendar will help you to do this. Don't get distracted by everything you have on next week, or even later this week—focus on what you need to do today, or right now. Having zoomed out and taken the time to plan, you should trust your plans and your schedule. You don't always need to see what is coming up around the bend; you just need to zoom out often enough to orientate yourself and anticipate the next few steps.

Use undated task lists

Capture low-priority actions in lists without committing them to a date.

As I have already stressed, one of the keys to managing actions effectively is to capture absolutely everything you may need to do, whether or not you are ready to schedule time for it. While I recommend the task list and calendar in Outlook as the best place to capture short-term actions, it is worth considering other places and tools to capture longer-term or 'nice to do' actions. These can be managed in undated task lists. Here are some ideas.

Outlook undated tasks

Outlook allows you to enter undated tasks that do not get allocated to a specific date but do show up in your master task list (see figure 1.3). This can be a good strategy to capture ideas or 'nice to do' actions. If you do use this strategy, it is important that you review the list on a weekly basis to consider if any tasks deserve to be date-activated.

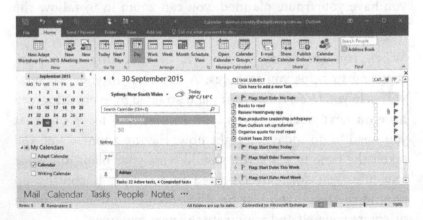

Figure 1.3: undated tasks in Outlook

OneNote

OneNote is a note-taking tool that comes bundled in the Office suite. While it is often used to capture and manage meeting notes, it can also be used very easily to capture lists under specific headings. Creating sections in OneNote for different projects or endeavours gives you a place to park actions and regularly review them.

OneNote can be used instead of undated tasks as a way of creating lists of actions that you are not ready to schedule or date-activate yet. For instance, I might want to create a list of jobs to be done around the house during the holidays, and rather than scheduling each job into Outlook, I could simply make a list in OneNote to refer to on my phone when I am ready.

Paper notepad

It would be remiss of me to not mention the good old pen and paper. I strongly believe that while your electronic calendar and task list will serve you better for your date-activated work, a simple page in a notebook can serve you well when capturing actions or ideas that are not date-sensitive. For instance, assigning a page in your notepad for each of your direct reports (or your manager) means you have a consistent place to capture things you need to discuss with them when you catch up. Just make sure you review these regularly so they are not lost or forgotten.

I often say to people that I *organise* myself electronically, but I tend to *think* on paper. I still use a paper notepad to sketch out ideas, sometimes take notes in meetings and make the odd list related to a project.

Capture mind clutter

Get it out of your head and into a place you can trust.

Your brain is an amazing tool in so many ways, but the one thing it does not always do well is remember things *at the right time!* It can hold millions of memories for a lifetime, but somehow it fails to remind you to pick up batteries when you are at the supermarket.

As the amount of information we need to hold on to increases, so too does our need for tools to help us to manage it. We simply cannot trust our brains to recall everything we need to do at the right time.

Trying to manage all these actions in your head leads to what I call *mind clutter*. A 'mental note' to remember to do something stays top-of-mind for a short period, but then gets buried under new thoughts. Because you tend to remember things by association, the thought will pop up again at some point, but often at the wrong time — when you are not in a position to complete the action.

You might need to send an email to a colleague. You make a mental note but promptly forget once you are back at your desk. Later that day you are in a meeting and your colleague is mentioned. By association, you remember that you had meant to send him the email. But you cannot send it now, so you make another mental note. And so it goes on all day, or all week. Each new mental note escalates your stress levels and mind clutter.

Now multiply that by all of the things that you are trying to remember but are successfully forgetting!

The key to managing mind clutter is to consistently capture the action in your centralised action management system when you first think of it. Get into the habit of moving it out of your head to a place that you trust, using one of the mind clutter strategies in figure 1.4. If it is a meeting or appointment that you think of, put it straight in your calendar. If it is a task that does not require immediate action, put it straight into your task list, preferably scheduled for the appropriate day. If you are concentrating on a piece of work and think of something new that you need to do, get into the discipline of flicking straight to your action management system, capture the thought and get back to concentrating on your work.

What about when you are away from your desk? Take advantage of the mobile technology you have at your disposal. If your smartphone synchronises with your calendar and task list, capture the action on that and it will sync back to your main system. If you cannot schedule the action then and there, at least make it visible in some way so you can process it later when back at your desk. Send yourself an email or leave yourself a voicemail. That way you will make sure it can be picked up again and scheduled properly. At the very least, have a dedicated place where you write mind clutter down. But if you do that, make sure you centralise it into your action management system when you get back to your desk.

MIND CLUTTER STRATEGY	RATING
SCHEDULE IT ⟶	Best
CENTRALISE IT ⟶	Better
CAPTURE IT ⟶	Good
REMEMBER IT ⟶	Bad

Figure 1.4: mind clutter strategies

One of my clients, the head of a large law firm, learned the value of this approach. He had been trying to remember far too much stuff. This worked well enough when he was a young lawyer and the workplace operated at a slower, less information-driven pace.

He was trying not only to remember but also to organise everything he needed to do—the emails he needed to send, the calls he needed to make, the discussions he needed to have. But now, as he was working to lead the organisation through massive change, drive the business forward, inspire his team with vision and still manage the small matter of his own workload with key clients, his head was no longer cutting it as an organising tool.

He realised that by getting all the things he needed to do out of his head and into one place he trusted, in this case Outlook, his mind was freed up to think! He had more mental capacity to create, plan and add value.

Tech Tips

Centralising all of your work by using one organising tool will increase your focus and your ability to prioritise your time and attention. You could use a paper diary to centralise your actions, but a more relevant and effective tool to use today is your email and calendar application, whether that be Outlook, Lotus Notes or Gmail.

Here are some tips for leveraging your technology to centralise your work.

- Use the electronic task list in Outlook, Lotus Notes or Google Calendar to create a consolidated list of all your priorities. In my experience, most people do not use this function and so miss out on a powerful way to manage their priorities.

- Harness the power of mobile technology to capture actions on the run. Enter tasks using the task function on your smartphone (make sure it is synced to your desktop task list in Outlook or similar). On the iPhone use Reminders. If using an Android device or a Windows phone, use Microsoft To Do or look into purchasing an app that syncs with your desktop system.

- Download an app such as Memo Mailer on your iPhone or Android device to capture voice-memos and have them sent instantly to your inbox. This is great for capturing mind clutter or ideas, and can also be set up to send the memo to your EA or one of your team.

- If using Outlook and OneNote, you can capture actions in your meeting notes in OneNote and send them straight to your task list in Outlook using the Outlook Tasks button in the ribbon toolbar.

- If you have been assigned an action in a channel in MS Teams, you can send the post to yourself as an email so that you don't forget to schedule the action into your task list. Look for the … when you hover your cursor over the post.

- If your team uses Planner to capture and assign project tasks, it should automatically generate an email to you with a link to the project task in Planner. This again should make it really easy to get the action into your calendar or task list in Outlook.

CHAPTER 2
Schedule it forward

To maximise productivity and ensure you are getting your work done in a timely way with the least amount of stress, you should try to work in the *proactive zone* (see figure 2.1).

As much as we want to work proactively, we frequently find ourselves working in two *reactive zones*. Far too often we end up reacting to incoming work such as emails, or leaving things until the last minute. Working in these reactive zones causes pressure and stress, which leads to mistakes and, arguably, a drop in the quality of our outputs.

Reactive zone 1—the first minute

If you react to incoming work by doing it straight away, there is a risk that in doing so you drop something more important. Allowing new incoming work to disrupt you will divert your focus from your existing work.

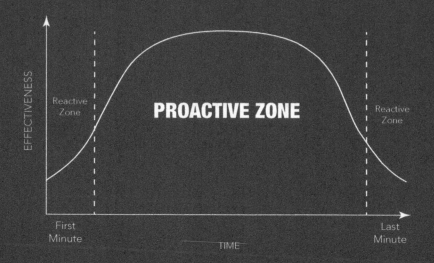

Figure 2.1: the proactive zone

There is no need to do every task the minute it arrives. Most tasks do not have that level of urgency. It is an illusion to think that by doing things the minute they come in, and getting them off your plate, you are working more effectively. I would suggest that the opposite is true: you are fragmenting your work and creating a level of reactivity that is unproductive.

Reactive zone 2—the last minute

At the same time, leaving things until the last minute is also highly reactive and can also create problems. When you let incoming priorities just sit in your inbox, or on your desk or in a list, they are at risk of drifting dangerously close to their deadline before you finally do them. Eventually they become urgent and can't be ignored any longer, so you end up reacting to these as well. Stress levels rise and work quality probably goes down. Not good for your blood pressure! This is often referred to as procrastination — putting things off to a later time even though you know this will have a negative effect.

Another implication of procrastination is that you will tend to cause reactivity in other people if you delegate work at the last minute. If you delegate a task to a team member, or even simply request information from someone at the last minute, you are creating unreasonable urgency for others.

One of the keys to working effectively in today's busy workplace is working as much as possible in the proactive zone. Ideally 80 per cent of your time should be spent in this zone. You will never totally escape the need to react to urgent work, and you will always end up leaving some things until the last minute, but no more than 20 per cent of your time should be spent in these zones.

Working in the proactive zone requires an action management system that facilitates what I call *proactive scheduling*—a date-activated task scheduling system that allows you to schedule actions on specific days. You can schedule priorities for today or tomorrow, or next week or even next year. This is critical for getting things done in a timely way. Ideally your proactive schedule will live alongside your calendar, so you can see your meeting workload and task workload for any given day. Outlook, Lotus Notes and Gmail all have the functionality to allow you to view your tasks alongside your meetings for the day or week.

It is also important that your proactive schedule allows you to reschedule tasks quickly and easily. In fact, most electronic systems will automatically roll a task over to the next day if it is not completed. It makes your work highly visible, as your tasks sit front and centre with your meetings, which allows you to plan your time holistically. You also get a better sense of priority, as you decide when you are going to focus on your most important tasks and you can sequence your task list in order of importance. Your electronic tools may also allow you to prioritise your actions using a simple High, Normal or Low rating.

By scheduling your actions and committing to a start date in this way, you are more likely to do the work before it hits its due date (i.e. work proactively). It will no longer just sit in the pile, hoping you will remember it!

Later we will explore proactive scheduling in more detail. The key thing now is to evaluate whether your current system is cutting it. Is it encouraging you to work proactively on your most important priorities, or is it causing you to work reactively, lurching from one deadline to the next?

Decide *when* and schedule

Allocate the resource of time to your priorities to work more proactively.

Possibly the most important question you can ask yourself about any action is 'When?' When are you going to set aside the time to work on that priority? Whether the work is an input that arrives in your inbox or is proactively driven through your own planning, it needs to get some traction in your busy and crowded week.

Time is the resource that fuels your actions and creates traction. If you do not allocate time to your actions, they can easily languish on a wish list somewhere. You mean to get to it, but time passes you by. If you leave it long enough, time eventually takes control and the matter becomes urgent. As the deadline closes in, the urgency increases and your hand is forced. As I have already said, I have often observed that urgency can often reduce quality and increase stress.

The key to managing your actions proactively is to manage the resource of time. Decide roughly when you will start working on your task, schedule it for the appropriate date and then manage any conflicting priorities that may arise. If you allocate your time in a reasonably balanced way, chances are you will find your work much easier to manage and will get more of it done proactively, before it becomes urgent.

As discussed in the previous chapter, when may mean a very specific time, with the activity scheduled into your calendar. A meeting is a good example of a very specific when. You may need to meet with some of your team to make a decision on an issue, so you schedule that meeting for 2 pm next Tuesday. You have set a very specific date and time and you protect that time by closing it off from other activities.

'When' can also be more flexible. You may decide to call a client next week to follow up on a project rollout. This is a more proactive task and could be done anytime next week. You decide to schedule it for Tuesday as you are in the office on that day. It may or may not get done on Tuesday, but that is when you will consider that task again, and either do it or reschedule it.

As illustrated in figure 2.2, a proactive schedule goes beyond a basic task list, which is usually just a 'vertical' pile of tasks, and schedules tasks for the appropriate date. This requires a centralised action management system that will allow both meeting and task workloads to be viewed 'horizontally' forward, day by day.

To create workload balance, these date-specific task lists should be displayed in the same view as your meeting workload so you get a complete view of your commitments and priorities for each day. Many will remember paper diary systems that allowed space for both meetings and tasks for each day. Today Outlook, Lotus Notes, Google Calendar and most other electronic systems will allow both tasks and meetings to be scheduled in this way.

Deciding when helps you to control the volume of actions that demand your time and attention. Time is a bit like a big, wide, heaving ocean. If we drift along in our little boat without aim or direction we could end up anywhere or nowhere. Or we can take control, set the sail and actively plot our course. Our schedule gives us that control.

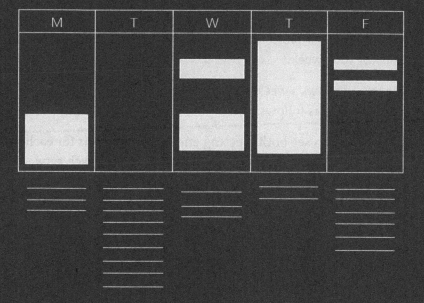

Figure 2.2: the proactive schedule

Plan your time using a weekly workflow

Zoom out of your schedule to see your meeting and task workload.

One option that can help you to manage your work more proactively is the weekly workflow view. This screen shows you a week at a time (many electronic calendars give you the choice of a five-day working week or a full seven-day view). Outlook, Lotus Notes and Google Calendar all provide this view of your week.

Figure 2.3 shows a weekly view in Outlook. The key features of this view are as follows:

- You can see both meeting and task workloads for each day and get a sense of the balance between each type of activity.

- You can clearly see when you have more capacity for working on your priorities.

- The calendar provides a place to schedule more 'fixed' work, such as meetings and bigger tasks.

- The task section provides a place for more 'flexible' work, such as tasks, priorities and discretionary work.

- Time blocked out in the calendar and tasks can be rescheduled quickly and easily by dragging to another time or date.

The weekly workflow view does not provide a lot of detail and therefore is not necessarily the best view to use when executing your plan. For this we need the daily plan view,

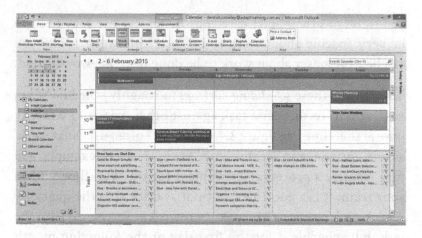

Figure 2.3: example of weekly workflow in Outlook

which we will look at in the next chapter. This view is best used when holistically planning what you need to do and when you need to do it.

Use action horizons

Use the horizons of next week and next month to defer less pressing actions.

You cannot do everything at once. You have to be realistic about what can be done today, or even this week. Being able to schedule tasks for future dates helps you to spread your workload and get into a proactive rhythm. But when you are moving quickly, it can be hard to make a decision about exactly when you will aim to complete some tasks. So you need to be able to capture absolutely everything that might need your attention, without getting bogged down by picking exact dates for everything.

With a proactive scheduling system you schedule tasks broadly and loosely when they are some way off, and more specifically and tightly as their start date approaches. So you may need to be very specific about work to be done this week, while you can be a bit looser about work to be done next week or beyond.

You can use these *scheduling horizons* to roughly schedule when you want to reconsider a task against other priorities you may have at that time (see figure 2.4, overleaf). I often use 'Next week' as one horizon, and 'Next month' as another. For example, you may identify a process improvement for the workflow within your team. It is a good idea, but not as critical as the quarterly reporting looming in the next two weeks. So you capture the task, but schedule it for the first day of the following month to reconsider it then. You are not scheduling it specifically for action on that date, but rather setting a date for it to come back onto your radar screen for review.

At one level this may feel like you are just putting stuff off and procrastinating, but it is a very necessary strategy when dealing with a high volume of competing priorities. In fact, you will see in Part III that scheduling work forward is actually a form of prioritisation. In this case you are prioritising it for later.

Managing your priorities is always a trade-off between what needs to be done and how much time you have available. Getting really focused about what you need to get done today or tomorrow or this week helps you to manage the balance between your priorities and your time. Using horizons is a simple but effective way to stay focused on doing the right work at the right time.

A note of caution: using this approach will probably mean that you will have a longer task list to consider on Monday, or on the first of the month. Make sure you factor that into your routine. On that day, quickly evaluate each action and decide when you

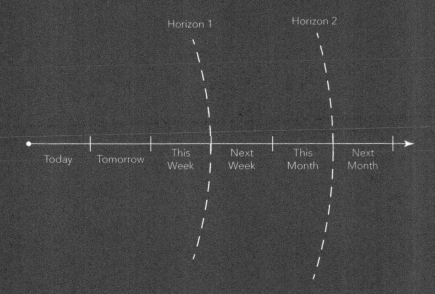

Figure 2.4: scheduling horizons

are going to do it. Should it be done today, or scheduled for some time this week, or rescheduled for next week or next month?

Focus on the start

Be aware of the due date, but manage the start date.

How many times have you heard or said, 'Focus on the deadline, everyone' or 'Don't interrupt me, I'm on a deadline'? So much of our work is deadline-driven, and as our deadlines get shorter we wonder how we will cope in the future.

The word *deadline* traces its roots back to the American Civil War. It is believed to refer to a line marked in the sand 20 feet outside of a Confederate prison camp. The guards were authorised to shoot and kill any prisoner who crossed the line.

I hope that missing a deadline in your role would have less dramatic consequences for you, but there is no getting away from the ubiquitous nature of deadlines in the modern workplace. The good news is that managing your deadlines is surprisingly simple. Don't focus on them! Focus on the start date, not the due date.

Consider how you might currently manage your work. An email arrives in your inbox, with an action and a deadline attached. Maybe the deadline is the end of next week. It is not immediately pressing, so you can safely leave it for the moment. As the days go by, you spot the email as you scroll up and down your inbox. Each time, you assess how close you are to the due date and consider whether you need to deal with it yet. Do you run the gauntlet, and leave it to the last possible moment? Are you now under pressure and hoping desperately that nothing else urgent pops up (something always does) as you try to meet the looming deadline?

Think about just how much pressure and stress that scenario causes you. When we focus on the due date only, we are not really in control of the work. We are just passively watching it until it reaches a point where it can no longer be ignored. From the moment it arrives to the moment we do the work we use up a lot of mental energy — even *before* we have begun physically working on it.

Let's try again, but this time focus on the start date. The email arrives. What would happen if when processing your emails that day, you acknowledge the deadline, and review your schedule to see when might be a good time to start working on that task? You consider roughly how long it will take, and also check your meeting schedule for the next week or so. You decide that Monday of next week would be a good day to schedule the task, as you will be in the office and have a reasonable chance of getting it done. That still gives you a few days' wiggle room if other commitments get in the way. You can now forget about the task until Monday but start to manage it forward from that point.

Focusing only on the deadline often leads you to ignore the more useful marker, the start date. Of course you may still end up doing this piece of work at the last minute, but more likely than not you will get to it in a calm, measured way before it is due.

Balance your workload

Create a balance between your meeting and task workloads.

To manage your time holistically, it is essential that you create balance between your meeting and task workloads.

It can be hard to create balance if you manage both of these types of work in different places. But when you bring them together using a single organising tool, you begin to see whether and when your work is in or out of balance.

One of the biggest challenges I see senior managers facing is 'protecting' time for their priorities. Because they often manage their meetings using a tool such as Outlook, and manage their tasks using paper tools, their time allocations tend to become meeting heavy. Lack of balance during our core working hours has become a massive issue over the last couple of years as online meetings have become more numerous. We are spending too much time going from meeting to meeting, with no space left for our other priorities. Unfortunately, the impact of this is we work longer hours to catch up.

You have only so much time available on any given day, so make sure you balance that time. Protect time for meetings and also for tasks. If you do have a full schedule of meetings, recognise that you will not get as many tasks done and avoid scheduling them for that day. Instead, look forward in your workflow and schedule tasks for the days with fewer meetings.

What if you feel that you have no control over what gets scheduled into your calendar? I see many people become 'victims' of their schedule, and feel that they have no choice. But we always have a choice. I believe that we need to become more ruthless about what we allow into our schedule, and that means we need to get comfortable with negotiating. We do not have to say 'No' to every meeting, but we should if we feel the meeting is not a good use of our time, or if we are not clear about the meeting purpose, objectives or our expected role. We can also negotiate about the timing of the meeting, or the length of the meeting.

Your time is valuable, and recognising the need for this balance is the first step to controlling your time.

Don't dilute your task list

If you want your task list to keep you focused, keep it focused.

Don't dilute your task list with unimportant items. Keep it for your priorities. If it becomes cluttered with non-essential stuff, you will not trust it.

Megan is a marketing manager in a large financial institution based in Sydney. After an initial coaching session, she was very excited about the prospect of getting her inbox down to zero, and committed to doing this by the end of the week.

Sure enough, on Friday I received an email with a screenshot of her empty inbox attached! Well done, I thought. A couple of weeks later, in our next coaching session, I found her a bit deflated. Her inbox was looking good, but her task list had turned into this big, red (overdue) and out-of-control pile. She felt like she had simply shifted the problem from her inbox to her task list.

This is often a natural side-effect of getting your inbox under control, especially if you are not yet proficient with managing a proactive schedule. Two things had caused this build-up of tasks for Megan.

Firstly, when excitedly disposing of her emails, she had turned a whole raft of reading emails into tasks, thus expanding her task list by diluting it with 'low priority' work. As these were not priorities for the times for which they were scheduled, they just ended up being rolled on from day to day.

Her second problem was that she was not distributing her priorities to future days and weeks but just letting them pile up for today and tomorrow. With a little bit of coaching, and a few tweaks, she was able to cull her task list and redistribute some of her work over the coming weeks. She ended up feeling much more in control.

Some of the principles we use to manage our meeting workload in our calendar can help us to manage our task list more effectively as well. For most people, the calendar is the place to go for specific, focused information about what we need to do and when we need to do it. We schedule our meetings for the appropriate time, and we rarely put meetings in our calendar that we are not attending. We do not dilute our calendar with non-essential information. We use it to keep us focused on our important meeting workload.

If you want your task list to keep you focused on your important priorities, apply the same discipline that you use for your calendar. Filter out low-value work before it gets onto your list. Don't use your task list as a place to 'park' non-critical actions just to get them out of your inbox, or out of your head. Your action management system should contain only your priorities — the actions that you have decided you need to invest time in.

So how should we manage non-critical actions? Where should we put ideas, reading and things that we should do if we had the time but that are not critical to our immediate outcomes? Try the following strategies:

- Keep a separate 'Consideration list'. This should be an undated list for non-critical actions that you review weekly. You can then date-activate actions when appropriate.

- Batch activities such as reading or processing approvals. Block out time in your calendar once or twice per week to review and batch the relevant information together in a folder.

- Have a dedicated place to capture ideas for review. This could be a notebook, or a page in OneNote or Evernote.

- Have a dedicated place to capture discussion items by person. This is useful for items that need discussion with your manager or direct reports, for example. Again, a page for each person in your notebook or OneNote is perfect for this.

Lastly, update your task list regularly to ensure it is not getting clogged up with completed tasks that don't need to be there anymore, or things that have changed in priority since you entered them. The more you keep your task list focused, the more it will keep you focused.

Next steps only, please

Schedule only next-step actions in your task list.

We all have projects that we are working on. Some are large and some are small. None should end up in your task list, though. Why not? Because you cannot do a project—you can only do the next step in a project. The next step might be a meeting or it might be a task. Either way, reserve your calendar and task system for specific actions rather than general chunks of work.

Many people make this mistake when they first start using a centralised task list to manage their work. They start using the task function in Outlook, and before they know it they have a pile of projects on their list, just rolling over from day to day with no sense of momentum and no clear next action. This creates clutter, confusion and a feeling that you are not making progress.

Every task should be defined as a clear next step, preferably starting with an action word. This will make clear what you need to do and, once completed, should give you a sense of progress.

Which of these provides the clearer picture of what needs to happen next?

Budget presentation

Call John Hancock re: budget slide changes

When you get into the habit of always scheduling the next step, you can begin to 'recycle' tasks and forward schedule the subsequent steps. Rather than mark the task complete, ask yourself 'What is the next step?' and simply change the subject and set a new start date. So, 'Call John Hancock' becomes 'Email new slides to John Hancock'.

This is a great way to keep work moving forward, and to make sure you don't end up procrastinating over big chunks of work sitting on your list. Projects do need to be managed somewhere, and in Part III we will look at some options for this. But your calendar and task list are where the rubber hits the road, and should contain only the next steps.

Track it back

Use your forward schedule to remind yourself about work or information due back from other people.

We have now looked at systems to help you manage what you need to get done. But how do you track what *other* people have committed to? As your next step often depends on other people getting work to you in a timely way, it is critical that you have a way of tracking not only what is due back to you, but when it is due back. You may need to track responses to emails, information requested for reports, work delegated or decisions made. And you may need to track these things across all the people you deal with, including your team, boss, peers, colleagues in other departments, clients and suppliers.

Not having a fail-safe system in place for managing work due back causes unnecessary reactivity. You request information for a report but simply manage that reminder in your head. This means there is a risk that if other people don't get back to you in a timely way, you may not remember that you have not received the information until you sit down to create the report. Would it not be better to remember that it is due back a few days before you need it? Or at least the day before?

Many people create other lists or piles to manage this type of work. For example, if emails require responses, they might create a folder called 'Response needed' and batch the relevant emails in this folder, reviewing the contents on a regular basis. Others simply make a list in their notebook. While these strategies are better than relying on your memory, they have one major flaw: they don't manage the *when*. These lists require constant review to determine if anything is due back and needs chasing. Unnecessary time and effort is spent going over the same information again and again.

A more efficient and elegant solution is to date-activate the reminder in your action management system. When you send the email or delegate the work or request the information, ask yourself when you need the information by, and then schedule a reminder task the day before. Label the task clearly as 'work due back'. That way it is really clear that this is something you are expecting from someone else rather than something you need to do.

Due — John re: updated data for monthly financial report

45

By scheduling the task for the appropriate date, you are managing the reminder proactively. You can forget about it until your system reminds you. When it does and you have not yet received the response, you can make a decision to chase it up or reschedule to another date and give the person a bit more time. Just as in your own task workload, some items will be more time-critical than others. Some things will need to be chased on the day; others might only need to be brought back onto your radar screen periodically.

A senior manager I once coached loved this strategy so much he enthusiastically shared with me that his team disliked me a lot. I was surprised, as I consider myself to be a reasonably likable guy. He gleefully told me that it was because of the 'track it back' strategy. They no longer got away with missing deadlines for work he had delegated. In the past he would delegate and forget, and they knew this. Now he seemed to remember everything, and would chase them relentlessly for the work they had committed to!

I ended up working with his team to show them how to manage their work proactively so they could meet his deadlines in a timely way. It was a win–win for everyone, and an example of a team that went from working reactively to working proactively by using complementary tools and systems to manage their work.

Information at your fingertips

Keep relevant information attached to the action in your calendar or task list.

You have so much information coming at you all of the time, it can be hard to find what you need quickly when you go to do a piece of work. The last thing you want is to have a priority scheduled in your list and then waste time looking for the related email so you can do the task. Ideally you should be able to find it quickly, without having to think too much about it.

It therefore makes sense to keep the information with the task, or with the calendar entry, so it is at your fingertips when you need it. Outlook allows you to schedule emails as tasks or calendar entries, and embed the email directly into the activity (see figure 2.5).

As you will see in Part II, this is one of the key strategies for getting your inbox under control. This gives you a certain freedom, as you can schedule your work knowing that the information is attached.

So, whether you are using Outlook, Lotus Notes or Google Calendar, spend some time learning how your system manages the conversion of emails into actions. In Outlook you can drag an email into your tasks folder to convert it into a task.

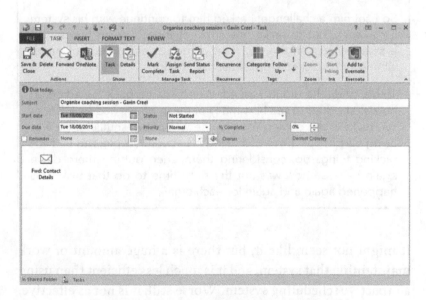

Figure 2.5: email-related task in Outlook

In Lotus Notes and Google Calendar there is a dedicated action button for converting emails. Get into the habit of scheduling this work into your system and stop using your inbox as an ineffective task list.

This seems like hard work

There are quite a few elements to get right in order to manage your actions in a proactive way. It takes a bit of effort and a bit of discipline. But let's look at the alternative. How much effort is involved in managing your work using fragmented 'piles'?

One of our clients was sceptical about making the required changes, suggesting that his system of printing out emails (yes, you heard me right), and stacking them in neat action piles on his desk, was more efficient than scheduling them as tasks. 'Less work involved as I just leave them on my desk until I do them. I don't have time to be scheduling them only to reschedule them each day', he said.

So I set him a challenge. I asked him to continue with his system for a week, but to make one small change. I asked him to put a small asterisk in the top right corner of each piece of paper whenever he picked it up. 'Trust me', I said.

To his credit, he did as I asked. When I came back, he admitted he was shocked to see how many of these pages had four, five or six marks in the corner. You see, he was paper-shuffling. He was using his piles as a way of making his actions visible, but he kept picking things up, considering them, then putting them down again because now was not the right time to do that task. This happened again and again for each email.

It might not seem like it, but there is a huge amount of work maintaining that system, and it is much less efficient than using a proactive scheduling system. Worse still, it is not as effective, and it leads to reactivity.

Before you say, 'That is not me', I would suggest that although you may not print emails out, you may scroll up and down your inbox every day looking for outstanding work. This is equally time-consuming and inefficient.

Tech Tips

Working proactively on the right tasks is one of the most effective productivity strategies available to you. One of the problems with using technology to create a proactive schedule is that most electronic task lists are geared towards managing deadlines rather than proactively managing start dates. Here are some tips to help you to use technology to work more proactively, focusing on the start dates.

- Set up a task workflow view in your calendar. In Outlook, open the Daily Task List and set the task sorting to By Start Date. In Lotus Notes or Gmail, go into settings and enable to-do's to be shown in the calendar.

- Convert emails to tasks or calendar entries in Outlook by dragging them to the task or calendar folder.

- Drag tasks from your task list into your calendar if you want to protect time in your schedule for the work. This is really useful when you are planning your week and what to get more specific about what you do at specific times.

- If using an iPhone or iPad, download Calendars 5 by Readdle to view, complete or reschedule tasks on the run. This app shows both your meeting workload and your task workload across the week, and synchronises with the calendar and reminders apps on your device.

- Schedule placeholders in your calendar a few weeks in advance to protect time for task workload or time to plan. Mark these appointments as Tentative so that other people who view your schedule know to discuss it with you if they need to meet at that time.

CHAPTER 3
Focus your day

Have you ever got to the end of a long, busy day at work, and felt like you haven't actually achieved anything you hoped to? It's a frustrating feeling. Maintaining focus in today's workplace is hard. Not only do you have more information and distractions coming at you than ever before, but you are probably working in an open-plan workspace and have lost the protection of four walls and a door.

But if you do not work out a way to stay focused on your commitments and priorities, the precious time you do have will quickly evaporate, leaving you wondering where the day went. Sound familiar?

Hopefully the previous two chapters have helped you get all of your actions scheduled in one place. Now we will look at some strategies that will keep you and your schedule organised and focused.

By planning your day, or your week, you are attempting to shape the future. You are trying to control as best you can what will happen, knowing of course that it will probably not work out quite as you would like it to.

To shape the day that lies ahead, you need to assess all the data currently available. What meetings do you have currently booked in? What are the existing priorities you know you need to tackle? What tasks are unfinished from yesterday or last week? What time do you need to finish your work day because of personal commitments? All this data gets fed into your daily plan, with the probable result that you have way too much to do in too little time. So, decisions need to be made and your time prioritised, with some items removed or rescheduled, until you have a reasonably realistic plan of action before you.

Start each day with a daily PASS

Get focused for the day ahead.

Each morning, spend ten minutes reviewing the day ahead and clarifying what meetings and tasks will require your focus. I call this my daily PASS, which stands for Preview, Add, Subtract and Sequence.

If your normal start-of-day routine is to go straight into your first meeting without time to review, organise and plan, or to open up your email and just plough in where you left off yesterday, you are setting yourself up to fail. You may not be fully aware of what is the best use of your time for that day. Of course you can never fully control your day. Unexpected things will come up. Priorities will change, but that does not mean you should not put a plan in place and fight hard to execute it.

Dwight D. Eisenhower, who served as a general in World War II before becoming the 34th US President, once said,

'In preparing for battle I have always found plans useless, but planning is indispensable'. He knew that once the first shot was fired, the battle plans went out the window, as his troops had to react to battlefield realities. But the time spent planning for the battle prepared him to make better decisions in the heat of the moment. The same idea carries through to daily planning. Your daily plan may not survive your first meeting, or the interruption you get at 8.30 am, but it will allow you to measure any new priorities against what you had planned to do, and to ask, 'Which is more important?' or 'Which is the best use of my time today?' Your plans must be flexible but have the resilience to withstand the constant pressure of everyday urgency.

One busy law firm partner I worked with described his usual pattern through the day like this:

Arrive at work, check emails from overnight.

Off to first meeting.

Back at desk before next meeting, check emails.

Off to next meeting.

Check emails . . .

Next meeting . . .

Check emails . . .

Next meeting.

You get the picture.

It wasn't until 5 pm that he finally had time to focus on his own priorities, and he often worked on these until 9 or 10 pm! As he described this pattern to me, I saw the realisation dawn on him that this was a crazy situation.

So we made a small change. We set Outlook to open up into his calendar, where he now managed his meetings and his tasks. He committed to putting a daily plan in place first thing each day, or just before he went home the night before. He scheduled two blocks of time to process emails during the day. And his new focus shifted to working this plan. When he came out of a meeting, he now looked at his list of priorities to work out the best use of his time before his next meeting. He focused on his priorities, rather than just trying to plough through a lot of noise in his inbox.

The following four-step daily planning process, illustrated in figure 3.1 (overleaf), will help you to quickly shape your plan:

1. **Preview** all of the actions and commitments that you have scheduled for today. Consider both your meetings and tasks. Get a general sense of your day to start with.

2. **Add** to your task list or calendar any actions that you need to focus on. You may need to review your inbox(es) to see if anything critical has arrived. Ask yourself the question, 'What else?' This will provide a full picture of what needs your time and attention.

3. **Subtract** anything that does not deserve to be there. Reschedule any items on your list that are not critical for today, or are not achievable today. Be realistic about what you can get done in the time available, and don't set yourself up to fail by scheduling too much into your day.

4. **Sequence** your task list from *most important* to *least important*. Consider first what is most important in your day, and sequence your tasks in this order. Outlook allows you to drag tasks up and down the list to create the desired sequence. (You might also

Daily PASS

1. **P**review
2. **A**dd
3. **S**ubtract
4. **S**equence

Figure 3.1: the four-step daily PASS

consider your energy levels, and the amount of time between meetings, when sequencing.) This sequence is not set in stone, but it allows you to look at your list and see the next most important thing you need to do. It can also be helpful to visually highlight the actions that are a 'must do' for today, as against your 'nice to do' tasks.

As you will see, this planning process is as much about what you will *not* do as it is about what you *will* do. It provides focus. Make this a habit, like brushing your teeth or checking your blind spot before you pull away from the kerb. Don't let a busy day get in the way of this habit. That is when you need it the most!

Without this focus you can easily become side-tracked and overwhelmed. So take ten minutes each morning (or the afternoon before) to review your priorities and set up your day for success.

Highlight the critical work

Measure both importance and urgency to define how critical your work is.

How should we prioritise our day-to-day work? How do we determine the best use of our time? In his ground-breaking book on productivity, *The 7 Habits of Highly Effective People*, Stephen Covey crystallised the idea of measuring work according to both its urgency and its importance. Every piece of work has some amount of each, so urgency and importance are reasonable measures to help us to work out what we need to do first, or next.

When we zoom into our daily plan, and we look at the list of tasks that we have decided are a good use of our time today, how do we work out which should be our first priority for the day? The most urgent? The most important? The quickest? The easiest? I believe there is no right answer to this question. Any of these could be correct at different times. It depends on how you feel, how much time you have before your first meeting, or even where you are based on that day.

As a general rule, though, importance should trump urgency, as difficult as that might feel in the moment. If we were to think about urgency and importance being lenses that we look at our work through, we should try to always look through the importance lens first, then the urgency lens. If we become disciplined at putting importance before urgency, our work will naturally become more proactive, and less of it will end up becoming urgent. Of course it will not stop other people making life urgent for us, but it will minimise our self-sabotage. We will of course also spend more time on value-adding work.

When we settle on our list of priorities for the day, we need a way of separating out the critical from the non-critical. If we can identify the few absolutely critical activities that we must tackle today, it will help us to better sequence our task list and to make the right decisions as our priorities change throughout the day.

In George Orwell's allegorical novel *Animal Farm*, the pigs who liberate the farm from the humans set up an idealistic, communist-style society with the mantra that all are equal. But in time some pigs take on leadership roles and indulge in the perks that came with this, eventually ordaining, 'All animals are equal, but some animals are more equal than others'.

My mum used to read that to me as a toddler as my older brother studied the book at school. Even at a young age I was captivated by the humour in this, as well by its sardonic truth.

The same may be said of our task list. All tasks are equal, but some are more equal than others. Some things need to be placed at the top of the list because they are urgent, some because they are important. Some because they are both. Some deserve to be highlighted as critical to today and therefore become must-do priorities.

Each day, try to identify between three and five tasks that you see as critical and that must therefore be completed. Highlight these tasks in some way so they stand out. Many task systems allow you to prioritise tasks as High, Normal or Low. Make the critical tasks High priorities.

Limit the number of high-priority tasks for each day, otherwise the priority ranking loses its meaning. The idea is to lift the few critical things above the rest to achieve more focus and clarity. Some of your chosen tasks for the day will be critical because they are time-sensitive and must get done. Some may be critical because they are important and you want to get them done proactively.

If your task system allows, consider sequencing your task list in order of execution, with the critical priorities at the top. Sometimes you may start your day with a few quick wins, or a task that is not critical but suits your location or energy level. But as a rule I encourage you to try to start your day with your most critical tasks. Get them out of the way early and the rest of your day is a downhill run. You will feel better, and will also be more able to deal with the changing priorities that every day brings.

Manage the change

Your plan will change — be ready to manage the change.

You may have planned a day that is productive and focused, with achievable outcomes, yet nothing goes as planned. Not all of the data is in yet. New work comes in throughout the day that cries out for your attention. Interruptions. Emails. Phone calls. Urgent requests. Client issues. These new demands will compete with your planned activities and risk throwing your plan, and your day, into disarray.

You need to learn to manage these changes in a way that creates a balance between urgency and importance. You can allow your plan to be derailed by a range of 'urgent' new priorities that arise through the day. Their apparent urgency calls for you to drop what you had planned to do in order to deal with the new issue. This is manageable if it happens occasionally, but if it happens all day, every day, your productivity will suffer. The result? The activities you had planned to do proactively become urgent themselves, throwing your schedule into further chaos.

To manage this tension, you should critically evaluate the importance of new incoming work against the importance of the planned work. Is this new work more important than what you were already trying to get done today? Which holds more value? Which is the better use of your time? You must then test the urgency of the incoming work. Is it urgent, and is the urgency real or false? Is this reasonable urgency, or has it become urgent because someone else has left it until the last minute? You cannot control how other people manage their work, but you can begin to set expectations and stop their poor planning sabotaging your own plans.

By getting into the habit of first evaluating importance and then testing urgency, you will start to make better decisions about what really needs to happen. You will respect your time more and have better control over your plan — the future that you shaped at the start of the day.

The reality is that there will always be new stuff competing for your attention and new pressures from different directions. Your plan will change as the day unfolds, but with the right mindset you can accommodate the changes and minimise disruption to your plan. Just as Eisenhower found that he made better decisions in the heat of battle when he had planned, you will make better decisions in your day when you begin with a plan.

Update the progress

Keep your task list up to date and stay motivated.

In his book *The Game Changer*, Dr Jason Fox writes about the *contextual momentum* needed to drive meaningful progress. Jason writes about 'crisp daily actions':

> May your actions be crisp and tickable!
>
> By crisp, I mean sharp and specific. And by tickable, I mean that it can be ticked off in a checkbox. It can be quickly and clearly assessed as done or not.

Keeping your daily list of actions up to date is key to feeling and seeing progress through your day. When you complete something, tick it off the list or 'recycle' the task into the next action. Then look at what is left on the list and ask, 'What's next?' This cadence will create traction and build momentum towards your goals and objectives. You will also feel more motivated as you see your list of actions get smaller through the day.

Like a project plan, your daily plan should be dynamic. It will change the minute it is created, and it is only useful if it is kept up to date. That said, don't be a slave to it. Some of my clients in senior roles only get to interact with their plan a couple of times each day, because of their heavy meeting workload. But having put the plan in place in the morning, they can hold their priorities in their head more easily. They might not get the chance to update the task list until the end of the day, but they still see and feel their progress.

Tech Tips

Focusing on your priorities can be a challenge when you have so many distractions threatening to divert your attention elsewhere. Here are some tips to help you use your technology to create that daily focus.

- Set up a dedicated daily plan view in Outlook, Lotus Notes or Gmail. Go to the day view, and ensure that you can see both your meetings and your task list for today.

- Change the settings to open to your calendar rather than your inbox. In Outlook, go to File, Options, Advanced. In Lotus Notes, right-click on the calendar icon and choose Set Bookmark as Home Page.

- Don't let incomplete tasks just roll over from one day to the next. Reschedule tasks to another day if you are not going to get to them or they are not a priority for today. To do this, open the task and change the start date, or drag the task to another date in the week view.

- Use mobile technology to keep track of your daily plan. Calendars 5 is a great app that combines your meeting and task workload on the iPhone or the iPad.

- Make the processing of emails and the checking of MS Teams channels a part of your day. Rather than being constantly distracted by these, allocate some time every hour or couple of hours to keep things moving for the people around you.

KEY PRACTICE
Prioritising

In the integrated productivity model (see figure D) we reviewed in the introduction, *processing, planning* and *prioritising* are the three practices or habits that drive the whole system.

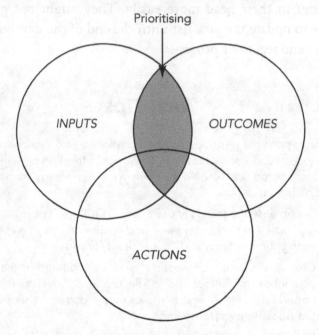

Figure D: the integrated productivity model—(i) prioritising

In the model, prioritising occurs at the intersection between Inputs and Outcomes, but the benefit of prioritisation can be most felt in your Actions system. Effective prioritisation ensures that you are working on the right actions, which should balance the reactive inputs we receive with the proactive, outcome-realising activities which we need to drive ourselves.

The word priority is rooted in the Latin *prioritas*, meaning 'existing or coming before in time, order or importance'. When prioritising our work we determine what precedence we give each action and therefore the sequence in which we do them. The problem is, this concept has become muddled and misunderstood over time. For many people, by saying something is a priority they really mean it is urgent. For others it simply means that it is important. When we collaborate with others, differing understandings of 'priority' can cause confusion.

Stephen Covey created a lasting legacy in his work on prioritisation, notably the priority matrix, which is a tool for deciding where we should focus our time and attention. This matrix examined the relationship between urgency and importance, and provided a framework that became the basis of most time management thinking over the past three decades. But the prioritisation framework he made popular is only one of three types of prioritisation that we should use every day to organise our work. Figure E (overleaf) shows how each type of prioritisation has a different focus, yet they all work together to keep you focused.

Filtering

Filtering is essentially the implementation of the prioritisation process that Covey employed in the priority matrix. When you decide to action a piece of work or not to action it, you are filtering. You are making judgements about what is a good use of your time and what is not. At its simplest level, filtering involves a yes/no decision. When checking your email, you are filtering. When you assess the value of attending a meeting, you are filtering. When you accept a delegation, you are filtering. If you filter well, you will ensure that only valuable activities get into your schedule, so that the main focus is on value. And the outcome is that you do the right work more of the time.

In Part II we discuss a filtering framework that will help you to process incoming emails and other forms of work.

Scheduling

Most people do not see scheduling as a form of prioritisation. But it is one of the most critical prioritisation techniques available to us. Time is one of your most limited resources, so deciding *when* you will schedule and action your work is critical.

	FILTERING	SCHEDULING	RANKING
DECISION	Yes/No	Now/Later	First/Last
FOCUS	Importance	Urgency	Combination
OUTCOME	Right Work	Right Time	Right Order

Figure E: three types of prioritisation

As we saw in chapter 2, making decisions about whether you do something today or tomorrow, this week or next week, helps you to control your workflow, and therefore your time. The decision is now or later, with the focus on the timing of that action. Doing this well will ensure that you do the right work at the right time.

A few years ago I was running a workshop for a group of busy lawyers. As we talked about the idea of scheduling our work forward and rescheduling tasks that have not been completed, one of the participants indignantly complained, 'That's cheating!' He felt strongly that a task must be done according to its schedule. But rescheduling is simply prioritisation in action. When our time runs out, we need to reschedule any unfinished tasks, otherwise we are just kidding ourselves. And that *is* cheating!

Ranking

Finally there is the ranking method—creating a list ranked in order from most important to least important. This is most useful when you need to sequence items in a list. For instance, you might rank the tasks in your daily plan to ensure that you start the day with your most important priority. We called this 'sequencing' when we discussed the daily PASS process, but it is the same thing.

In the same way, you might rank a bigger-picture list of priorities for the month ahead. Simple project task lists just need to be listed in this way rather than being entered into a full project scheduling tool. Ranking involves first-to-last decisions, with the focus on the order of execution. If you do this well you will be doing the right work at the right time in the right order.

Prioritisation is more an art than an exact science. It combines many value judgements and should balance urgency against importance. Other people with their own sense of what is urgent or important will have a different interpretation. It is worth putting some thought into how you embed these three types of prioritisation in your routine.

Hybrid Help: Actions

Moving to a hybrid style workplace has created some unique issues in how we need to manage our actions and our time. We may not have realised it, but working in a common workplace with our managers and our colleagues gave us a kind of structure that kept us on track. Or at least gave us a nudge if we were falling behind, focusing on the wrong things, or delivering poor quality work.

Of course, that is still true, even if we are working from home or from a different location. But one of the key issues I witnessed when people started working remotely as a result of the COVID outbreak was the challenge people experienced staying focused, and particularly staying focused on the right work. This was not helped by the fact that the volume of emails we had to deal with increased as a result of remote working, and so did the number of virtual meetings. Here are some hybrid hacks that will help you to stay focused on the right work, wherever you are working.

The one constant

While you may not always be in the same location as your team, and may work from different workspaces through the week, the one constant that you have is your organising system. If you fully embrace MS Outlook as your one, consolidated organising system, and you are using Office 365, as long as you have access to a PC or laptop your meeting schedule, task list and email communications are at your fingertips.

I personally work from many locations. I work from my office, and sometimes I work from home. I work at client sites and I work in hotels. Recently I spent three months working from Italy with my European clients. In all of these locations I had everything I needed to stay focused and organised in Outlook and OneNote on my laptop.

If you still rely on paper notepads, sticky notes, printed-out documents or even a paper diary, you expose yourself to the risk that the information you need to do your work is in a different location. Very frustrating I would imagine.

Avoid back-to-back-to-back meetings

In a hybrid workplace where not all of the team is within line of sight of their manager, or each other, it is easy to fall into the trap of overusing online meetings as a way to stay connected and maintaining control. But the increase in meetings in our calendar comes with a cost. Workers are becoming stressed, overwhelmed and unable to get key priorities done during core working hours because of the volume of meetings they are expected to attend.

This is leading to working longer hours than before, as the only time they can catch up on other work is after dinner. So, although they might have less travel time because they are working from home, they are working a longer day. Add to this the practice of cramming back-to-back-to-back meetings into our schedule, and you have a recipe for disaster.

Do yourself a favour and protect times in your day or week that are meeting free zones. And give yourself at least a few minutes break between one meeting and another. Research conducted by Microsoft in 2021 demonstrated that attending back-to-back virtual meetings led to a decrease in the ability to focus and engage. A short ten-minute break between meetings helped the participants to be far more effective in each meeting.

Do a calendar audit

If you are finding that a lot of your time is being eaten up by meetings that other people insist you attend, try doing a calendar audit.

Look back over your schedule for the past four weeks. Review every meeting you attended and ask yourself how good a use of your time each meeting was. Were you needed in the meeting? Was it well organised and did it achieve clear outcomes? Was your time wasted?

Make some notes as you go and look for the patterns. Now, look at your meeting schedule over the coming four weeks. What decisions will you now make as a result of the hindsight you now possess from looking back? What future meetings should you cancel out of? What meetings lack a clear purpose and at least deserve an email to the organiser to request they specify the purpose and expected outcomes?

We can sometimes be a victim of our schedule, and we need to stop and do audits like this every now and again to ensure we are spending our time in the best possible way.

Switch on in virtual meetings

One of the things that I know irritates a lot of people in online or virtual meetings is the fact that many people do not turn on their cameras. Sometimes there are legitimate reasons for this, but often it is so the meeting participants can 'hide', probably catching up on other work or emails during the meeting. I have a fundamental problem with this. Don't be a *passive spectator* in meetings, be an *active participant*. If you decide that the meeting is a valid use of your time, then engage. Ideally you should make contributions and ask questions, but even if you do not do that, at least turn your camera on and be seen.

This is a cultural issue in many teams, and is a behaviour that should be led by the senior people in the team. If you don't turn your cameras on, then don't be surprised if your team don't.

Manage your time in 'Thirds'

I am a great believer that you can get a massive amount of work done in twenty minutes if you are focused and purposeful. This idea was cemented for me one day when one of my mentors called me on the fact that it took me nearly half a day to write my bi-weekly newsletter. He suggested that was way too long to spend on it, and I should be able to write it in half an hour! I baulked at this, and said it was impossible. But then I tried it, and low and behold, I had a pretty good newsletter written in about 30-minutes.

He was right. By limiting the amount of time I allowed myself, I was more focused. I have since mastered this concept and have gotten it down to twenty minutes. In fact, I have begun to think of a twenty-minute timeslot as a 'third', as it is a third of an hour (see Figure F).

The extension of this is that I now rarely have meetings for more than twenty minutes. I was inspired by Winston Churchill's character in the television series *The Queen*, as he explained to Her Majesty in their first meeting that he never had meetings for more than twenty minutes, as he had never come across an issue so complex or hard that it could not be resolved in that time. I love this, and again, it is all about being focused and purposeful. Everyone is more focused when you know you only have twenty minutes.

So, that is the mindset for getting stuff done. What can we achieve in twenty minutes? More than we think! I will talk more about this idea of 'Thirds' in the Hybrid Hacks sections further on in the book.

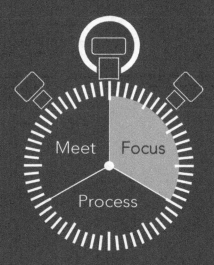

Figure F: managing your time in thirds – (i) focus

Focus your day when working at home

Finally, this is a hack that is very close to my heart. When I do work from home, I can be more prone to procrastination and distraction. I love cooking, and don't mind a bit of cleaning, so sometimes these quick chores that I could do divert my attention from the important priorities that I should be doing. Before I know it, I am putting on a wash, or hanging a picture on the wall. That is fine sometimes, and one of the clear benefits of our new hybrid working circumstance. But it is a problem when we are using these odd jobs as a way of avoiding the work we should be doing.

I find that putting a plan in place at the start of the day, and working to that plan helps me to stay focused and on track. The Daily PASS process that I outlined in chapter 3 is a great way to set your day up for success.

PART II
Organise Your
Inputs

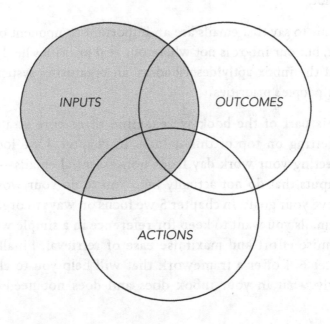

As discussed in Part I, work reaches us through many disparate channels, including email, meetings, interruptions, messages and phone calls. I call these *inputs*. An input is any communication, piece of information or potential action that lands in one of your 'inboxes'. It is your job to assess these inputs and determine which are and which are not worth keeping, and which might need action and which don't.

The volume of information we are now required to review each day borders on the ridiculous. Sometimes hundreds of emails and alerts compete for our attention. This volume of information has increased for many as a result of the move to remote and hybrid working. Unfortunately, many of us have become conditioned to this and have fallen into the trap of thinking that it is our job to respond to every email instantly. It is not.

It is fair to say that emails are an important component of our work, but our inbox is not where our real priorities lie. I once heard the inbox aptly described as 'an organising system for other people's priorities'.

In this part of the book we examine three core strategies for getting on top of this deluge. In chapter 4 we look at protecting your work day from non-essential emails — that is, inputs that do not actually help you to do your work or achieve your goals. In chapter 5 we focus on ways to organise the emails you want to keep for reference in a simple way to minimise effort and maximise ease of retrieval. Finally, in chapter 6, I offer a framework that will help you to clarify exactly what in your inbox does and does not need your time and attention. The result: an empty inbox at the end of each week!

Getting in control of your inputs will free you up to spend more time on your core work. Your stress levels will drop and your feeling of control will increase.

CHAPTER 4
Reduce the noise

You will have sensed by now that one of the key themes in this book is the goal of working more proactively and less reactively. This means reducing the urgency, which in part depends on reducing the attention we give to non-essential things coming in — that is, *noise.*

The high volumes of noise filling our inboxes, workspaces and heads make us more stressed and more likely to work reactively. You might feel that you cannot control what is external to you, but you *can* manage it to minimise its negative impact.

The volume of noise will creep up over time if you let it. Like weeds in a lawn, it needs constant attention. But if you are diligent and you pull a weed whenever you see one, it is not hard to keep up. The same goes for email noise. Whenever you spot it, do something about it. Investing a small amount of your time in weeding your inbox will save you a lot of time over the weeks, months and years.

Then go beyond the inbox and try to spot all of the other forms of noise that stop you concentrating on your important work.

Reduce email noise

Minimise the noise coming into your inbox.

As we receive ever greater amounts of email, the amount of noise we receive will also increase. This is not limited to spam or junk. It takes many forms — some externally driven, some internally driven.

One of my clients described his inbox management like this. He said he was pretty good at managing the absolutely critical stuff, like client emails, and he was also pretty ruthless with the absolute rubbish and junk. 'It's the middle that's killing me', he said.

For him, a big contributor to the problem was the build-up of emails that were purely for his information. These emails made his inbox a more stressful place to visit than it really needed to be.

I helped him by suggesting that there are three types of emails we will generally receive:

1. actionable emails, which require a response or an action from us

2. informational emails, which may or may not be of value to us

3. questionable emails, which add no value.

As shown in figure 4.1, some of these will be needed, some will be simply noise.

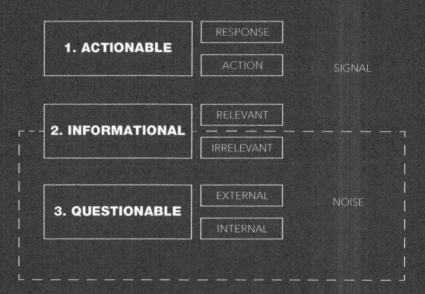

Figure 4.1: types of emails

Actionable emails

Actionable emails are the most important emails you receive, and they need to be managed well. They may just need a response or may require a more comprehensive action. Some are urgent and need instant action, and some can be dealt with at a later time. You definitely need these emails, and as discussed in chapter 1, they should be managed using your task list and calendar.

Informational emails

Informational emails may take the form of reports, group messages, newsletters, status updates or CC emails. Some of this information will be relevant and important to you, but some may be of little or no value. The irrelevant emails are the beginning of your noise problem. If you receive too many of these, you begin to lose sight of the important stuff.

You can easily set up rules to automatically file informational emails. Use the Rules editor to create a rule to file and batch regular newsletters, non-essential reports and system emails. Block out time in your calendar to review these emails daily or weekly as necessary. If you have executive support, ask them to screen your inbox and delete or file non-essential emails for you.

Questionable emails

These low-value emails also fall into two categories. Unsolicited or unwanted external emails, often called spam, include marketing emails and the like, or even hoax emails. These relentlessly fill our inbox and take time to delete each day.

You may also receive solicited junk. This might include external marketing emails that you signed up for, or even internal distribution-list emails that once were relevant but now add no value. Maybe you've switched roles but are still on distribution lists that keep you 'in the loop' on what is happening in your former area. Useful then, not so much now. I must confess to still receiving several emails a day related to a committee I was on several years ago. I really should get off that distribution list. The problem is, the voyeur in me likes to keep up with the gossip. Interesting, but totally unproductive!

Some questionable emails may be internally driven by your colleagues, and come in the form of CC emails and Reply All conversations. When other people are not thoughtful about what emails you need to be included in, the volume of noise can grow for you. If you receive a high volume of this type of noise, it is worth talking to your team and creating some team agreements around how and when you use functions like CC and Reply All. The problem of email noise is a cultural issue in many teams, which I talk about in detail in my book, *Smart Teams*.

Here are some strategies for dealing with questionable emails:

- Add them to your Junk list. You can easily divert emails that you identify as junk to the Junk Email folder by using the Junk button in the Ribbon toolbar in Outlook.

- Unsubscribe from newsletters and distribution lists that add no value.

- Report spam to your IT department. They have the tools to block this at the server level.

- Let your team know what you need to be copied in on.

- Encourage your team to reply to the originator in an email conversation, rather than always replying to the whole group.

Turn off the alerts

Turn off email alerts on all devices and check email proactively.

What would happen if we could hear other people's thoughts? If every time someone somewhere thought something that was about us, or even mildly involved us, we heard it in our head. What if we heard things that were actually nothing to do with us at all? While at first blush this might seem interesting and appealing, the reality of it would be quite stressful. I would imagine it would be very distracting, and ultimately unproductive. Now I don't believe that thought transference and mind-reading are possible, but I do sometimes wonder if email alerts cause a similar problem.

If every time you receive an email you hear a *bing*, see a sliding notification on your screen or feel a vibration on your phone, you are letting other people's thoughts enter into your consciousness and grab your attention. Email alerts are designed to distract you to get your attention. This distraction can occur hundreds of times a day, and while sometimes it is useful to see when a particular email comes in, for the most part the interruption is of little value; it just breaks your concentration on more important work.

Research suggests that the intrusion of constant email alerts causes a loss of focus and can lead to our concentration work taking one-third longer to complete. We stop and start our work all the time because of these interruptions, and this has a negative impact on our productivity.

Most people know at some level that allowing emails to interrupt their day is not productive but allow it to happen anyway. Why is this? Firstly, there is an element of *fear*. Fear of missing something urgent, especially from our boss or from a key client. In this case, we need to ask ourselves if we are just supporting their poor email habits. Email should not be used to communicate urgent directives. For anything urgent I would suggest they should pick up the phone or come and see you, as they often do anyway.

We also yield to *curiosity*. We want to see what's coming in just in case it is more interesting than what we are doing now. There is always the chance of an opportunity, a crisis or some juicy scandal that we don't want to miss.

But I believe the main reason we allow ourselves to be side-tracked is *habit*. Email alerts are turned on by default in Outlook. A few years ago (when we might receive 20 emails a day) this did not distract us too much. But now that many of us receive 100 or more a day, it is a problem.

If this is the case for you, kick the habit. Turn your email alerts off for good—on your desktop and on your mobile devices. This will allow you to build a productive new habit of focusing on your work while still staying on top of your inputs.

Then build a routine around your email. Check it at regular times, and when you are not checking your email, put it out of your mind and ignore it. You will be more focused, get more done and work more proactively as a result.

Still worried or concerned about the risk? What if you miss a critical email? Most email systems allow you to set up rules that will alert you if you receive an email from designated people or with a specific subject line. For example, an executive assistant might set up a rule to alert her if her boss emails her. This might be necessary, as her boss might email from a meeting requesting that a report be printed and delivered to the meeting room.

Most of us do not have this sort of urgency in our role though, so try to manage your emails without *any* distractions first, then decide if there are any exceptions that should be dealt with differently. We need to question the effectiveness of some of the poor habits we have built up by default over our careers.

I was shocked one day when delivering a presentation at a prominent Sydney consultancy firm. I had recommended that the participants turn off their email alerts so they would not be unnecessarily distracted from concentrating on their important legal work. One of the consultants said that he could not do that. The senior partner in his division had mandated that they respond to every client email within ten minutes!

Now I am all for good customer service, but that seemed to me to be way over the top. They had to be constantly monitoring their email 'just in case', which would have had a dramatic impact on their ability to concentrate. Worse still, they were teaching their clients that however minor the communications, they could always experience instant gratification, thus shaping the clients' expectations while creating a rod for their own backs.

In my view, good customer service is not about an instant response — it is about a timely, high-quality response. I want to know that the consultant is concentrating fully and I am sure every other client would feel the same way. That said, of course we would want them to respond quickly in exceptionally urgent circumstances.

Every time I run a training session or give a conference presentation, I get a huge amount of pushback when I recommend turning off email alerts. People know it is coming, yet still they groan and sigh. 'Do we have to?' Yet one of the most frequent pieces of feedback I get when I meet people after the training is,

'I can't believe how much more focused I am now I have turned off those alerts!'

Check email proactively

Build a proactive routine around checking emails.

Email was designed as an asynchronous communication tool. This means you can send the email and the recipient can read it at a different time. Meetings, phone calls and conversations are examples of synchronous communications. They happen simultaneously for all involved. The power of email is in the fact that we can deal with incoming work in our own time. But increasingly over the past decade email has morphed into a synchronous communication tool. The sender now often expects that you will read their email and respond to it immediately.

If you have made the smart move and turned off your email alerts, you will need to proactively review and process any mail that has arrived since you last checked. Building a proactive routine around your email helps you to maintain a healthy balance between being responsive and focusing on your current priorities. Your incoming emails have the potential of becoming future priorities in your schedule, but they should not always jump to the head of the queue in front of your current work. When is the best time to do this? How often should you check?

How frequently you check emails will depend on your role. Some roles do require a constant awareness of what is coming in and, for many emails, immediate action. But be careful before you let yourself off the hook here — these roles are few and far between. Most workers and managers do not need to check email constantly to do their job effectively. They only like to think they do because it brings a sense of control into what often feels like an out-of-control environment. New email also generates a feeling of excitement in an otherwise routine day. Maybe there's good news, maybe bad news — *any* news is more interesting than the report you are working on!

One strategy to break this cycle of reactive email-checking is to build a proactive routine and communicate your intentions to those around you. Firstly, you need time to properly process your emails each day. Without this the volume will build up and you will fall behind. Aim to put aside two, maybe three blocks of time during each day to process your emails. First thing in the morning and late in the afternoon are ideal times, with maybe a slot at lunchtime if necessary. I believe you can get by quite comfortably with two processing times each day, especially if you have reduced the noise in your inbox and are decisive when processing. The main aim when processing your emails during this time is to make decisions about what needs to happen with each email, and we will cover this when we discuss processing in the feature at the end of Part II.

Outside of these processing times, I recommend a five-minute check of your emails about once per hour. This can be done between meetings, or on completion of a task, and should involve no more than a quick check to deal with anything urgent, and maybe delete and file a few emails. This keeps you in touch with what is happening, but on your terms. The rest of the time you should be focused on your current work, priorities and commitments.

To begin with, you may need to schedule your main processing times in your calendar. This will help to support your new habit and avoid giving that time away to meetings. View those time slots as necessary daily maintenance and protect them well. Communicate your routine to others, and set the expectation that if they send an email, you will deal with it in a timely way but you may not see it immediately. Let people know that if something is urgent, they need to communicate it to you in a different way — through a phone call, a conversation or maybe a text message — to get cut-through. Most people will understand and respect the need for this, as no doubt they are suffering from the same time pressures that you are!

Batch information emails

Batch information emails such as newsletters and non-critical reports to be reviewed later.

A certain number of information-only emails in our inbox is unavoidable because while we consider some of this to be noise, some information emails are useful and valuable, although not time-critical. Newsletters are a great example of this. Because they have no time-sensitive action associated with them, we often leave them in the inbox where they build up and cause noise and distraction.

A huge volume of information arrives in our inbox every day. It is pushed at us from news services, subscription services, organisational systems, our colleagues, our boss and our friends. Everyone is sharing information, which seems like a wonderful thing at first glance, but the problem it creates is a glut of reading that we can't possibly keep up with because we don't have the time.

It is essential that you don't let information messages build up in your inbox and stop you getting on top of the really important emails that require action. The question is, where should you put them? You probably don't want to create a task for every newsletter that comes in, and simply filing them may mean you never go back and look at them.

A simple strategy is to create a folder called 'Reading'. This type of filing folder, which I call a *batching folder*, is designed to collect emails together in one convenient place. These should be kept separate from your archive filing folders, which are for emails you have finished with but you want to keep just in case you need them later. The Reading folder is a 'live' folder that you review on a regular basis.

Once you have set up your Reading folder, you can use either a manual or an automated strategy to direct relevant mail into the folder. Drag information emails into this folder when you are processing your emails or, better still, set up a rule to automatically direct them into the folder when they arrive in your inbox. If there is a consistent or unique characteristic in the email, you can easily build a rule around it.

For example, every week I receive a Google email with a summary of articles posted on email productivity. This content is invaluable to my thinking on email management but is not time-sensitive. So I have set up a rule to automatically divert that email into my Reading folder. When I travel for business, this is the folder I go to on my tablet to catch up on this content. This means I deal with non-critical but useful information on my terms, in my own time.

Now a few words of caution. Firstly, if the newsletter does not add value, get yourself off the mailing list rather than just moving it. Secondly, if you have made the effort to move stuff to a Reading folder, make the time to actually read it. I find that blocking out 30 minutes on a Friday in my calendar is a great way to keep up with my reading if I have not had a chance to do it while travelling.

Lastly, you may receive certain emails that are automatically generated—reports, approvals, notifications and the like. It may also be useful to batch these in their own folders, such as Approvals or LinkedIn invites. Again, these emails can be manually or automatically moved into folders and you can set aside time in your calendar to deal with them. Try not to create a batching folder for every email, though. As with so many things, less is more.

Delete decisively

Don't be afraid to delete.

A new culture is creeping into today's workplace—the culture of keeping absolutely every email we have ever sent or received. Information is power, but too much information can become noise instead of knowledge. At times it seems like our determination never to be caught out is consuming our time, resources and brain power.

I have worked with many executives who never empty their Deleted Items folder. It is a filing system of sorts. It often surprises me that people never empty this folder, and end up with thousands of emails just sitting there. I often wonder if these people ever empty the bin in their kitchen. Or do they keep the rubbish in their cupboard just in case?

We need to get back to making sensible decisions on what we keep. If it is not worth keeping, delete it. Be ruthless. They are just emails, and once you have read them or actioned them you will probably never need them again. Be ruthless with the obvious rubbish. Of course, there will be certain emails you do want to or are obliged to keep, even though you know you will probably never need them. No problem. Deal with them quickly and simply by *filing* them.

There is a line with 'keep' on one side and 'delete' on the other. Where do we draw it? If you can work that out roughly to begin with, it will make it easier to make a quick decision when processing your emails.

Here's what I do. I keep almost anything of note from my clients, except simple 'thank you' emails. From my team, I only keep emails informing me of something noteworthy, confirming a decision or that I need for record keeping. With personal emails, I keep only those that contain useful reference material. Other than these, everything else gets deleted.

For the most part, our focus should be on bigger things than managing historical conversations. So do some critical thinking, set your decision-making parameters and make fast decisions. You may get a few wrong, but mostly you will be right.

Tell them to SSSH

Manage other people's expectations and buy yourself some time.

Somewhere over the past few years expectations in the workplace shifted. The people we communicate with went from expecting responses to communications within a day or two to expecting to hear back within an hour or two — and in some cases, within a minute or two! They now send emails and then chase us for a response almost immediately. The instant nature of email has accelerated the pace of communication, and it is putting immense pressure on all of us. For email to be the productive tool we were promised, we must learn to manage expectations around how it is used, and how quickly we can deal with the requests and queries piling into our inbox every day.

One reason why email senders chase you up so quickly is they don't trust your inbox. Their experience with many of their colleagues is that their email disappears into a black hole where it gets buried in the pile of a hundred other emails that have arrived that day. They know that, as in advertising, they need to get cut-through, so they follow up their email with a call, an interruption or, heaven forbid, another email.

Their fear is that you won't see their email or, if you do, you will forget to act on it in a timely way. They are not picking on you—they have just come to expect this from everyone, including perhaps even themselves. You need to change this perception and manage their expectations. Telling them to SSSH is a great way to do both (see figure 4.2, overleaf).

When you receive an email that requires action, but that cannot be done immediately or is not a priority for right now, use SSSH to set a clear expectation about the work and when you will be able to do it.

Send a timely acknowledgement

Respond to the email in a timely way—the same day if possible. This need only be a brief response that acknowledges receipt. If you check your email regularly as a part of your email routine, you should be able to get an acknowledgement off within a couple of hours. If you have a busy meeting agenda it may be towards the end of the day. Remember, your response is not doing the work; you are simply acknowledging you have received the message.

Tell them to SSSH

Send a timely acknowledgement

Set an expectation about when

Schedule the action

Hold yourself accountable

Figure 4.2: SSSH

Set an expectation

Provide a rough estimate of when you might be able to do the work. This will help manage their expectations and make them feel comfortable that the work will be dealt with in a timely way. If the timing is not acceptable to them they can negotiate, but in my experience they will be okay with your timing more often than not. They understand that you are busy and will usually appreciate the clear communication. By doing this you are also buying yourself some time and will feel less pressured into simply reacting.

Schedule an action

The next step is to schedule a task or block out time in your calendar to make sure you do the work at the appropriate time. Don't set expectations with others and then forget. Get it into your schedule so it is visible to you and gets done.

Hold yourself accountable

You now have the responsibility for delivering on your promise. If you cannot deliver on the promise, put your hand up and renegotiate. Don't bury your head in the sand and hope that they won't notice you are late. Reset their expectations.

In the modern workplace, where everything is urgent and the expectation is 'as soon as possible', we need to re-educate those we work with and help them to trust us again. The new agreement should be that we will deliver in a timely way, but in turn they should request work in a timely way, not at the last minute. SSSH is all about building that trust. Over time the people you work with will feel comfortable with your work style and will hassle you less.

Reduce the disruption of interruption

Manage interruptions by being 'in the zone'.

Most of us need more time to focus. Not all the time, but at least some of the time. It is hard in our modern, interruption-driven workplaces, though. People, phones, emails and our own thoughts interrupt our concentration constantly. If we don't have a strategy for managing interruptions, our day becomes incredibly fragmented and we lose focus. Just as a car engine is less efficient in stop-start traffic than on the freeway, we lose productivity when interrupted too often.

We have already talked about email interruptions. But what about all the other interruptions we encounter? We often allow people to interrupt us as we feel the need to be polite, especially in an open-plan workplace. Add to this phone calls, MS Teams chat and social media alerts from platforms such as Yammer or Facebook. A lot of people feel that interruptions are out of their control, but there are things you can do that will give you that control back and help you to be more disciplined.

To manage interruptions we, and the people around us, need to understand what *mode* we are in at any given time. Do we need to concentrate to stay reasonably focused, or are we open to interruption? It is essential to maintain our awareness of which mode we are in, because if we do not, how can we expect others to know?

I believe there are three modes that require different responses to interruptions. These are shown in figure 4.3. The first is *lockdown mode*. In this mode, you need to ensure that you are not interrupted at all, because this is when you should be working

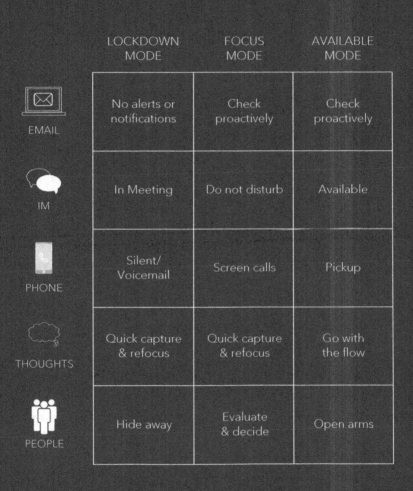

	LOCKDOWN MODE	FOCUS MODE	AVAILABLE MODE
EMAIL	No alerts or notifications	Check proactively	Check proactively
IM	In Meeting	Do not disturb	Available
PHONE	Silent/ Voicemail	Screen calls	Pickup
THOUGHTS	Quick capture & refocus	Quick capture & refocus	Go with the flow
PEOPLE	Hide away	Evaluate & decide	Open arms

Figure 4.3: modes to manage interruptions

on the mission-critical work that needs your full concentration and focus. You should reduce the temptation for others to interrupt you, and your temptation to allow it. The best way to do this is to shut your door (if you have one) or remove yourself from your usual workspace. Book a meeting room, hide in a quiet corner or a cafe. Get away from where you are most often interrupted — your desk.

Lockdown mode should be used sparingly and should be planned ahead in your calendar. Identify the tasks each week that really need concentration and block time in your calendar for uninterrupted work. Think about when you are going to do that work, and where you need to do it. Be sure to book the resources you will need ahead of time, and honour this commitment when the time comes.

The second is *focus mode*. The bulk of your discretionary time should be in this mode. You still want to be productive and should try to minimise interruptions. But in this mode you are open to some interruptions, although each one should be evaluated against what you are working on.

Evaluate the interruption quickly and ask yourself, 'Is this a good use of my time right now? Is it more important than the work I am currently doing?' Take a minute to assess the interruption and determine whether it is critical to right now. If not, defer the matter until later. Check your schedule and agree on a time with the person concerned. Help them feel that their issue will receive your attention, but just not right now. This approach will improve your focus during most of the day while you're at your desk and trying to get stuff done.

The third is *available mode*, when you are completely open to interruptions. In fact, I'd even go so far as to say you might invite interruptions during this time. Remember, interruptions are not inherently bad. They are a way of getting work done, and a lot of your work, as well as other people's work, is progressed through these interruptions. We can't rid the workplace of interruptions altogether. What we want to do is to try to minimise those that are unnecessary or unproductive.

Advertising some time during your week when you are 'in available mode' gives your team a time when they know they can check in, speak with you and share concerns. If you are a manager, it might be useful to say to your team, 'I am available at these times during the week. If you've got anything you need to bring to me, and it can wait until then, please come and discuss it at that time. My door will be open.'

Interruptions are just another form of incoming work. Learn to evaluate them quickly and respond appropriately, rather than reacting blindly.

Tech Tips

As the volume of information that pours into your inbox increases, so does the noise. And the noise will defeat you unless you harness the power of technology to fight it. Here are some tips to fight the war against noise.

- I have said it already, but I will say it again. Turn off your email alerts. On your desktop and your phone. In Outlook, go to File, Options, Mail and turn off the four default alerts. In Lotus Notes, go to File, Preferences, Mail and untick the three email alerts. In Gmail, turn mail notifications off in Settings.

- Set up email alerts for key people by right-clicking on an email from that person and going to the rule editor. Set up a rule to alert you when they email you. This is better than having alerts for every email.

- If you are using MS Outlook, turn on the Focused Inbox by going to the View Tab on the ribbon toolbar. This will sort your emails into two separate tabs. Your Focused Tab will show the emails that are sent directly to you or to a limited group, are from real people and will definitely include any internal emails. The Other Tab will show emails that have been identified as sent to large groups or as marketing emails or newsletters. The great thing is you can then teach the system what is focused or other by right clicking on emails and choosing the appropriate option. Once a day I will quickly review my other tab, and then press CTRL+A and Delete to clear those emails en-masse.

- Use email Rules to move non-essential emails into filing or batching folders. Outlook has a rules wizard, as does Lotus Notes. Gmail allows you to use tabs to manage less critical email, or to filter similar emails into folders.

- Add emails to your Junk folder in Outlook by right-clicking on the email and choosing Junk, Block Sender. Gmail allows you to move emails to Spam, or even to report spam so they can block it before it gets to you.

- If you organise a lot of meetings, set up a rule to auto-file meeting acceptances and declines. You probably do not need to see these when they arrive, and can always go to the meeting in your calendar to see who is coming.

CHAPTER 5
Keep it simple

I talked briefly in the last chapter about the need to keep emails. We use email to do so many things and we cannot recall everything said in them, so we have to keep a wide range of emails. You need to make the decision about what is worth keeping and what is not.

For me, the question is not so much about *what* you keep, but about *how* you keep it. How much time and effort is involved in keeping these emails, and in finding them again? I suspect a lot more than you might realise!

To avoid wasting time, it is imperative that we set up a simple filing system, one that is relevant to the needs of the modern workplace.

Most people need to keep some emails related to their role in a personal filing system within their mailbox. There is no need to grant other people access to these emails or to file them in a central filing system. This is personal stuff that they feel they may possibly need again at some point.

Some people are also required to file emails into a central group filing system. For example, many law firms and consulting firms set expectations that emails related to projects or clients are filed in a central document management system. This means many different people may be filing emails into the system, and many different people may need to find emails in the system. This complex scenario, requiring a whole-of-organisation approach, is beyond the scope of this book.

The strategies outlined in this chapter are designed to help people set up simple filing systems to serve their own individual filing needs.

Simplify your filing system

Consolidate your filing system to speed up your email management.

In every workshop I run I conduct an informal survey of the percentage of emails my participants feel they ever go back to again after filing. Most believe they refer back to less than 5 per cent of the emails they keep (many suggest it is more like 1 per cent). That suggests to me that 95 per cent of our email filing is a waste of our time. The problem is, we don't know which emails fall into the 5 per cent, so we tend to keep a lot just in case.

To be truly effective, we need to remove the friction from filing to make it quick and easy. Of course we should also make finding emails again more streamlined so we don't waste time there either.

In my experience, most workers use one of three types of filing structures to file their emails (see figure 5.1). The first is a *complex* system, which uses multiple folders in a structured hierarchy to store and organise emails. The second is a *condensed* system,

What's your email filing system?

COMPLEX $\longrightarrow$ Many folders

CONDENSED $\longrightarrow$ A few folders

COMPACT $\longrightarrow$ One folder

Figure 5.1: three types of filing system

which uses a handful of broad folders to manage emails. The third is the simplest of systems — just one *compact* filing folder to store all emails in one place.

As counterintuitive as this might seem, all of my experience with email has led me to conclude that the simpler your filing system is, the quicker it is both to file and to find emails.

Complex filing systems

Most people tend to use complex hierarchical filing systems. This is a hangover from the days of paper filing and the need for highly organised systems to manage large volumes of paperwork. I estimate that more than 80 per cent of people I have worked with over the years have used unnecessarily complex filing systems made up of many, many folders. These systems are often hierarchical, with folders, subfolders and sometimes even sub-subfolders! In the worst cases, every project, client, teammate, function, department and aspect of their role has a folder.

I believe that these complex filing systems can significantly hinder our productivity and offer little return on the investment of time we put into managing them.

Complex filing systems slow us down at two points — first when we file an email, and again when we need to find an email. Once we have decided that we need to keep an email, if our filing system is complex, we need to spend precious time working out:

Which folder should I put it in?

Does it deserve to go into two different folders?

Do I need to create a new folder for this?

Do I have a folder for it already? I can't quite remember!

All of these questions just to file a single email! Remember, 95 per cent of the time you won't ever need to refer back to that email, so that's a lot of questions to ask for something you will probably never need again. If you want any chance of keeping your inbox under control, you need to create a simple system that facilitates easy decision making, so emails can be filed and retrieved quickly and easily from any of your devices.

Complex filers can be very protective of their system and will cling fiercely to their logical approach to organising information. It is how they have always done it, and they do not trust any other way. But with encouragement, and some skill development around using the email Search function, many find they can simplify the system and still access emails easily. We will cover some search strategies in the next section.

Condensed filing systems

A less complex option is a condensed filing system — ten folders or fewer. Decide on a set of broad categories that allow you to bring together related emails, and base your ten folders on these. For this strategy to work, you need to decide which areas of your role really require a folder to manage the information. Looking at your existing folder structure, which folders could be amalgamated into one broader folder?

A client in a recent workshop had 21 direct reports so he had a heading folder called 'Team'. Underneath the Team folder he had a subfolder for each of his direct reports. Every time he got an email from a team member, he'd put it into that person's folder. If he got an email from another team member, he'd put it into their folder.

When we talked about this, he came to the realisation that he could probably achieve exactly the same result by just having one Team folder, filing all emails from his team into that one folder and then sorting his emails by person. This is an example of chunking up—essentially using one folder instead of 21 folders to manage the information. Have a really hard think about each of your folders and work out which ones deserve to be maintained, which might be deleted and which could be condensed and consolidated and into fewer folders.

Having a few broader folders works well when you have emails that need to be batched together and looked at as a group. In most situations, when tracking information we are looking for a single email. But sometimes we need to find a group of emails and a search is not so straightforward. Bringing multiple emails together as one group is more difficult than finding a single email. They could be from different people with different subjects and could have arrived at different times. There may be no obvious common factors connecting the emails, making them hard to group easily. In this situation a folder may work better, but these folders should be reserved for the true exceptions.

Later in this chapter we will look at some strategies to make emails more 'findable', which will help when you do need to find a group of emails rather than an individual email.

Compact filing systems

At the opposite end of the continuum from the complex system is what I call the *compact filing system*. This is filing at its simplest, using just *one* filing folder. As crazy as that might sound, this is far and away my preferred filing system. I personally made the switch from a complex filing system to one filing folder about ten years ago, and have never looked back. I went from 65 filing folders down to a single folder literally overnight. I have never regretted that decision. It increased my productivity enormously because suddenly filing was a really quick and easy process. Do I need to keep this or not? If I don't need to keep it, I delete it. If I do need to keep it, I file it.

When I file, I don't have to think too much about it. It doesn't matter what device I'm using. If I'm working in Outlook, it's easy to drag it into my filing folder. If I'm on my iPhone, I can just put it in my filing folder. It is easier to file this way on a mobile device because I don't have to scroll down a list of 50 different folders. I just have one. I believe it speeds up my email processing enormously. I probably keep more than I need to. But I am comfortable with that. It takes me about half a second to delete an email and about half a second to file an email. Really, keeping it doesn't cost me anything more than not keeping it. So I'll delete the obvious stuff but if I think there is any value at all in keeping it, I file it. And if I need to find an email in my filing folder using the Search function, it is as quick and easy as it was to file it in the first place.

One-folder filing is a pretty scary concept for a lot of people. When I've run sessions on this idea, it seems to polarise the crowd. Half of the people immediately go, 'No way! There's just no way that I could do that'. Their resistance is usually linked to one key fear. That is, if they put all their emails into one folder, how on earth will they find anything again? They believe that without structure and folders it will be too hard to find the critical email when they need to. I actually think the opposite is true. My experience working with thousands of executives over the years has led me to conclude that people who use one filing folder find things almost three times faster than people with complex filing systems. I will discuss this in more detail shortly.

Deciding if folders are needed

So how do you decide which system best suits your role? How do you work out if you need folders and, if so, which folders you need? The risk/searchability matrix shown in figure 5.2 is a useful way to work out a system that suits your individual needs.

In figure 5.2 the vertical axis measures the risk involved if you couldn't find that email. The horizontal axis measures the 'searchability' of an email—how easy it would be to find an email using the email Search function. Some emails are going to be really easy to find because there's certain information about that email that is known to you, or unique. For instance, you know it's come from a particular person, or the subject line of the email is standard and/or you can be confident that certain keywords would show up in a search.

If an email is high risk and might be hard to find, it may deserve its own folder. (But be very selective when making this decision. The more folders you have, the more time filing and retrieving will take you.) If an email is low risk and would be easy to find, it definitely does not need a folder of its own. If it is high risk but easy to find or, conversely, hard to find but low risk, you will need to make a judgement call. In both cases, I would urge you to trust your search tools and skills and do without a dedicated folder. You will be able to find the email. Obi-Wan Kenobi's advice to Luke Skywalker in *Star Wars* was, 'Trust the force!' My advice to you is, 'Trust the search!'

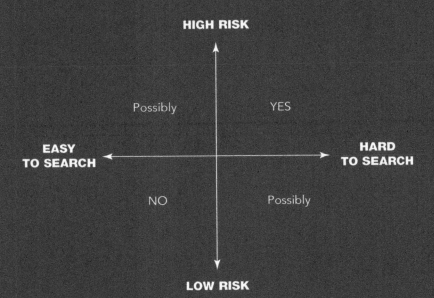

Figure 5.2: the risk/searchability folder matrix

Learn to search

Brush up on your search skills and save time when filing and finding.

Up until recent times, libraries were probably the most sophisticated and complex examples of structured, analogue filing systems. A library contains hundreds of thousands of books, which necessitates a reliable system to catalogue and find books quickly and easily. Several different systems are in use in libraries around the world, but probably the best known is the Dewey Decimal Classification (DDC). This system allows users to determine, first, whether a book is held in the library and, if so, its shelf location. It is complicated and requires that library staff have a deep understanding of the system. Users also need some level of understanding of how to locate a book using the system, and rely heavily on correct cataloguing information for each book.

Recent innovations have seen the introduction of automated systems that can find and retrieve books for the user. The user searches for the book in a database and enters a request. A robotic machine that can move both vertically and horizontally between the shelves then moves quickly and efficiently to the exact book location and retrieves it. Each book has a small wireless chip inside the cover that helps the robot locate it and later return it to exactly the same location. Amazing. If only we had such technology available to help us find emails!

But of course we do. It is called the email Search function. We just don't take advantage of it enough, or trust it (or ourselves) to find what we want quickly and effortlessly. I believe we need to adapt and stop wasting time on low-value activities such as organising emails in folders. As the size of our inbox keeps increasing, we can no longer trust our brains to accurately remember where we put things. We need to pull ourselves into the 21st century when it comes to filing by learning to use search tools that, just like library robots, will zoom off at our command and bring back what we want in seconds.

Search techniques

If you think about it, putting emails into folders is a search technique. In this case, you are building the search before you have filed the email. Each folder should then contain all of the emails that meet the folder's criteria, which helps you to find them when you need them. The problem with this method is that it is rigid and allows the emails to be stored only under one criterion — the name of the folder. This system relies heavily on our putting emails in the right folder to begin with, and on our logic not changing in the time between filing the email and looking for it again. If we put the email in the wrong folder, or forget which folder we put it in, we are in trouble. It's a bit like the Dewey system.

Moving to simpler filing structures increases flexibility. With fewer folders, you file the emails more broadly, then build a search to find the email if and when you need to. Searches can be incredibly flexible, allowing you to search by person, subject, keyword, attachment or any number of other criteria.

In my experience most people don't really know how to search and don't realise just how powerful their search tools are. Most people think, 'I'm not going to be able to find anything if it's all in one folder'. But in fact, as I've argued, the opposite is true. If you embrace the power of Search, you will find emails far more quickly. Let's examine some strategies that can help you retrieve information.

Basic search

The starting point for finding emails is to learn to use the Search box. Over the past few years most email systems have developed very powerful and effective search capabilities that most people do not take advantage of. Many systems, including Outlook, Lotus Notes and Gmail, have index search built in. This means that your searches will be very fast and comprehensive. Indexing organises your information in a way that makes it quicker and easier to retrieve when you need it.

Google uses indexing as a way of speeding up searching on the Internet. Similarly, when you receive or send an email in Outlook, it will be indexed, which makes it highly searchable. When you do a keyword search, it won't just search the 'To' or 'From' fields. It will also search all the address fields, including CC and BCC. It will then search the subject line and the body of the email. Finally it will search the name of any attachment. Some systems even search within the attached document for your keyword.

So to find an email in a single-file folder system often involves no more than a basic keyword search. There is usually something about the email that we can remember — the sender, the subject line, the company name mentioned in the body or the name of the project. While many people worry that they won't be able to remember the details or find the email without folders, I find this is usually not the case. Often these same people are perfectly comfortable searching for emails in their Sent Items folder — a single folder with thousands of emails in it. Go figure! It is usually not the system holding us back, but our mindsets. And our mindsets have sometimes been influenced by a few rare instances when we got burnt by not being able to find a crucial email. So we complicate our lives and our systems to avoid the risk.

Refined searching

Sometimes we need to go beyond these simple search techniques to find the email. This is where we can bring in the big guns and use the Advanced Search tools built into all modern email systems. Advanced Search allows us to refine the search criteria to narrow down the results. Essentially it allows us to search within a search.

I think of the Advanced Search function as a 'triangulated search'. Just like satellites triangulate to show your location on GPS, refining your search by two or three criteria triangulates to find your email quickly and accurately.

You might need to find an email from a colleague, but you know you have hundreds of emails from her in your folder. You guess that she may have mentioned the project name in the subject of the email, or at least in the body, and you also know it had a PDF document attached. Using this information, you can use the Advanced Search function to refine your search, and direct the search to show only emails that meet the criteria. If you don't find the email first time, you can tweak the search and try slightly different criteria. Remember, you are likely to need to find less than 5 per cent of the emails you keep, so even if it takes a few minutes to find the email, you have still saved time because your filing strategy was so efficient at the front end.

So have a look at the Search toolbar in your email client (see figure 5.3). Have a play with it. Find the Refine functions. Test it out. Get comfortable with using search and it will become your best friend if you let it, saving you much time and energy that can be spent on far more productive pursuits.

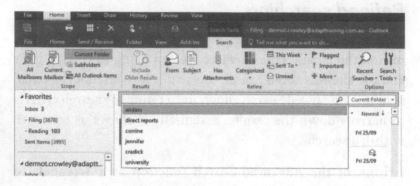

Figure 5.3: refine search toolbar in Outlook

One of my coaching clients, James, was appalled when I first suggested he ditch his 150 filing folders and use just one folder. Eventually he agreed to try out a simpler system of ten folders for a while.

Six months later I was delivering a presentation in the same organisation, and he happened to be in the audience. As I went through my logical argument for just one folder, his colleagues all folded their arms and dug their heels in. 'No way', I heard them mumble.

With this, James stood up and told them that he had had the same reaction six months earlier, but had tried out using ten folders. Since then he had consolidated further to three folders, and was now considering resorting to just one. This was a powerful endorsement from one of their senior colleagues.

One of the audience asked what had shifted for him. His response? 'I learned to use search!' His need for multiple folders had decreased as his ability to search had increased.

Make important emails easier to find

Reduce the risk of losing critical emails by increasing their findability.

We keep most emails 'just in case' and require nothing more than good search skills to find them if we ever need them. In most cases, if we could not find it at some future time it would probably not be the end of the world. So it is not worth wasting too much time or energy on cataloguing these emails.

But there are some emails that are worth managing a bit more carefully. They are more critical to our role, contain information we will definitely need to refer to, or have an element of risk involved that means we need to be sure we can find them, and find them quickly, if necessary.

For these few emails, and it should be just a few, it might be worth using one of the following strategies to make them more findable.

Use a dedicated folder

As much as this pains me to admit it, sometimes it is useful to have more than one folder. So if you have emails that are particularly critical, or you need to batch certain emails together for archiving as a group, then a folder might be the best solution. Not more than ten, though!

Rewrite the subject line

Subject lines do not always make sense or clearly describe the email they belong to. They become diluted as they are forwarded on, and we get lazy with them. Outlook allows you to click straight into the subject line and edit it. You can give the email a more suitable subject, save the change and then file the email. This will make your searches far easier.

Categorise the email

Outlook allows you to categorise emails. You can create your own categories and then apply these labels to each email. This colour-codes the email and also allows you to search easily by category. A word of warning: don't get rid of 50 filing folders and replace them with 50 categories. I use only two categories to label particularly critical emails. One is for emails confirming a speaking or training date in my calendar, and one for client testimonials and feedback. One of these is managing risk, and the other is simply making it easier to find disparate emails for marketing purposes.

Use these strategies judiciously and they will serve you well. You probably don't need to use them all — pick one and go with that. Everything else you need to file that is not critical should just go into your filing folder.

Take the pain out of archiving

Keep your mailbox lean and mean.

Our mailboxes usually have a size limit, although some organisations are now moving to unlimited mailbox sizes with an auto-archiving feature built in. If you are using Office 365 your emails probably archive automatically to the cloud when they reach six or twelve months of age.

In most cases, we cannot just keep on receiving new information and expect to be able to store it all in our mailbox. Massive mailboxes cause your IT department a lot of headaches and work, so they set limits. They send emails that warn you of your gross negligence (I love the irony of them sending you an email to tell you your mailbox is too big). They block your email until you reduce your mailbox size. For most IT departments the problem is not just the cost of storage space but, more importantly, the cost and time involved in backing up these mailboxes and restoring them if there is a major crash.

It's not just IT that benefits from your having a small mailbox. Your system will run faster and your searches will be more responsive when your mailbox is kept to a reasonable size. And it's frustrating spending precious time deleting old emails each day because you have received a notification to say that your mailbox is full. So archiving old emails, as well as calendar appointments and tasks, is a good idea.

Think of your mailbox as your home, and each folder as a room. You can move an email from your inbox to a filing folder, but you are not saving any space in your house. You are just moving it from one room to another. You need a garage to store the old stuff you want to keep long term but don't need to access very often. That is your archive.

Here is the problem though. You do not have time to waste on archiving. It needs to be either automated or so quick and simple that it does not become a chore that you procrastinate over. Remember, there is little value in spending a large amount of time organising history. The real value is in spending time organising the here and now, or the future. See archiving as necessary maintenance, but try to make it as pain-free and simple as possible.

Your organisation may have a formal email archiving system in place. If so, learn how and when to use it. If the archiving of emails is automated, find out where they go to and how to access them if you need to. Learn to search in your archiving system so you can find things quickly. And, as with your filing system, keep your archive as simple as possible.

If your organisation does not have an archiving system in place, you may need to set up a set of personal folders outside of your mailbox in which to archive emails. Most email systems allow the creation of folders that do not take up space in your mailbox. Again, check with your IT department for their recommendations. Many organisations have strict protocols about archiving emails to ensure the data is backed up and secure, and archiving to personal folders has become a very antiquated way of managing email storage since cloud storage became main place.

File on the run

Set up your mobile devices to allow quick filing on the run.

There is nothing more frustrating than having state-of-the-art technology at our fingertips, and yet still feeling like we are duplicating work and wasting time. If you are a busy executive who spends much of the day running from one meeting to another, most likely you stay up to date with emails through the day using your smartphone or tablet.

When you are out and about, using your mobile technology, you probably read emails quickly to keep an eye on what is happening, and respond to the urgent ones. But then you leave them all in your inbox! That means that when you do eventually get back to your desk, you need to go through it all again, trying to remember what you have read or actioned. I am struck by the fact that most people don't file emails using their mobile devices. They simply review, respond and leave them for later. Why is this? I reckon it is usually because they don't know how to file using a mobile tool and their filing system is too complicated to bother trying to use on such a small screen.

I think I might have already made this point (a few times), but a simple filing system in your desktop email system means a simple filing system on your mobile tool as well. It is so much easier to file an email on a mobile device if you have a simple filing system. Your smartphone or tablet can access your filing folder(s) in your mailbox in Outlook or Lotus Notes, allowing filing and retrieving.

So take every opportunity to file as you go, and delete as you go — on the train going into work, between meetings or waiting in the coffee queue. Take advantage of the micro-moments in your day, and experience the bliss when you get back to your desk and all those emails have gone away!

Tech Tips

In my opinion, way too much time is wasted on organising emails that we are finished with but feel we need to keep 'just in case'. Keep these emails by all means, but don't waste too much time in doing so. You will probably never need them again.

Here are some tips to help you to keep it simple.

- Keep your mailbox lean and mean. Even if you have the ability to automatically archive old emails to the cloud, it is a good idea to delete as much of the junk and rubbish as possible.

- To convert quickly from a complicated filing system to one or a few folders, simply set up your new folders, then go to each old folder and press Ctrl+A. This will highlight all the emails in that folder. Drag them into your new folder, and do the same with each old folder. You should be able to consolidate in less than 30 minutes.

- Learn to file using your mobile device. Many emails that you see on your phone can be deleted or filed there and then. Most people know how to delete on the phone. Extend that to filing and you will find you are facing fewer emails in your inbox when you get back to your desk.

- Set up categories in Outlook to tag the few critical emails you need to make more findable. Open an email and press the Categorise button in the ribbon toolbar.

- If you have decided to use one filing folder, you can set up a Quick Step in MS Outlook to file the email directly into this folder with the press of a button.

- If your Outlook mailbox has a built-in Archive folder (if you are using Office 365 you probably do), you can use this as your single filing folder. The benefit is that you will already have an Archive button on your Ribbon toolbar that allows you to file the email with the click of a button. The other benefit is that if you are using the Outlook app on your phone for email management, you can set up the swipe function to delete an email when you swipe in one direction, or file the email into your archive folder if you swipe in the other direction.

- If your organisation is using Office 365, you will have an online portal where you can access the online version of Outlook. This can be handy when you need to search for emails that have been archived, and you cannot find them in your mailbox. Often a search online will be more accurate with older emails.

CHAPTER 6
Process to empty

I believe that one of the most powerful productivity behaviours you can adopt in the digital age is to build the habit of processing your inbox to empty on a regular basis. Merlin Mann, a US-based blogger and productivity expert, coined the term 'Inbox Zero'. He recognised that the usual response to receiving more and more emails is to let them pile up in our overflowing inboxes. Through his productivity blog '43 folders', he started to promote the concept of going all the way to zero. While he did not invent the idea, he has been a pioneer in popularising it over the past ten years.

It seems to me that when it comes to email, many people resist the need to change their mindset and behaviours, and will often persist with poor habits that cause them stress and anxiety. Few process to zero on a regular basis. While many will happily go close, some just can't seem to finish the job of emptying their inbox! We all have a comfort line, and if we can get our emails down to that level, we feel in control. For some it is a hundred, for some it is a screen's worth of emails, for some it is ten.

I would argue for setting your comfort line at zero. You don't have to reach that line every day, but at least once a week you should be able to process all the way to empty. Of course, it is always going to be a temporary state. More emails will keep coming in, ruining your perfect white inbox, but that is not the point. Inbox Zero is not about never having an email in your inbox; it is about the power of being able to get yourself up to date on a regular basis. So what is it about this number that is so powerful? Why does zero make you more organised than ten emails in your inbox?

Firstly, processing all the way to empty means that you have made decisions about all of your inputs, and worked out which need action and which do not. You are completely up to date, which brings clarity. It should also mean that your actions no longer sit in a messy and confusing pile, but have either been done, or scheduled and prioritised for the appropriate time. There is a massive difference between an email marked for your attention sitting in your inbox, and an email that has been turned into a task or action and has been prioritised and scheduled.

Numerous studies suggest that workplace stress can be closely linked to our inbox. I have observed in my work that when many people get to zero, they feel in control and their stress evaporates. One client described the feeling as like a weight being lifted from her shoulders. Of course, being close to zero will achieve much the same, but going all the way provides a sense of satisfaction that is so, so worth it.

That final push to zero once a week ensures that nothing is left behind, that procrastination has been banished, and that nothing will slip through the cracks. By forcing ourselves to make a decision about what to do with every email, we create traction and a next step. Leaving it in our inbox just creates clutter.

The true power of zero was brought home to me several years ago when working with a high-profile CEO in Sydney. I had received a call from his executive assistant, asking me to come and work with him on his email management. This CEO was one of Australia's best-known business leaders; he had also been a sporting legend in his younger days. I was just a bit nervous! I remember walking into his big office thinking that I had better know my stuff!

He was a very organised man, as many top-level executives are, but email was the proverbial thorn in his side. He just could not get his head around how to manage the incessant flow. He had about five thousand emails sitting in his inbox, many of them unread. He got straight to the point. 'I hear you are the guy who can help me get my email down to zero', he said. 'I am sick of this, so what is the quickest way to get to empty?' 'Well', I shot back, 'the quickest way to get to zero is to just press Ctrl+A and then press Delete'. As the words left my mouth I realised he had taken me seriously. After a couple of quick clicks on the keyboard he said, 'Great, what's next?'

'Oops', I thought. He had actually done it. He had ruthlessly deleted his entire inbox, including that day's emails! On my advice! I suggested anxiously that he not touch anything and try pressing Ctrl+Z to retrieve them all. What he said next made me really understand the power of zero. 'No', he said, 'this is good stuff. One of the things I have learned about my inbox is that it helps me to be a *manager*, but it is getting in the way of me being a *leader*'.

Wow! The power of that thought hit me immediately, and I have been reminded of it many times since. For that CEO, email was blocking him from doing his most important work and he was not afraid to address that problem ruthlessly. I knew that, given his role, if there had been anything critical in his inbox, people would have come back to him, and he would have been at little risk of getting into trouble. But his unhesitating decision showed leadership, resolve and a commitment to action.

My view is that if we do not adopt a process-to-empty mindset, a part of our attention will always be caught up with the undecided business in our inbox. This distraction creates a barrier and a level of ongoing stress that we cannot afford in today's busy workplace.

Most of my clients are not high-profile CEOs, but I always ask them the question, 'What is your inbox getting in the way of?' You might wonder if that CEO built a new habit after his radical start? He did. He started again with his email, setting up a new system that allowed him to stay on top of it so he could spend less time monitoring his inbox and more time leading his team. I still find that inspirational!

So, how do we achieve this nirvana? Try the following strategies to get you to zero in no time.

Treat your inbox like your letterbox

Understand the one true purpose of your inbox.

The first step on the path to a healthy relationship with your inbox is to understand its purpose. Its one and only purpose is to receive emails. Treat it like the letterbox in front of your house, which is used only to receive letters and not as your document filing system. Similarly, your inbox should not be used as a filing system for old emails. If you need to keep emails, file them in a folder, but don't mix up filing with new emails.

Would you leave bills in your letterbox, hoping to remember to pay them? Of course not. You take them out and bring them into the house, where hopefully you have a system to manage them. So don't leave emails that need action sitting in your inbox. Get them out of your inbox and into a system that is designed for action management. Schedule them as a task, or schedule time in your calendar.

When you confuse the purposes of a tool such as your inbox, you end up not doing anything well. This means you don't action your work, file your information or manage your email flow as effectively as you could.

Clear the backlog quickly—the Mount Rushmore technique

Don't let your backlog stop you from getting on top of your current emails.

If your inbox is overflowing as you read this, do not despair. All you need to do is clear the backlog, and the backlog is easy.

The worst inbox I have come across had 72 000 emails in it. Seventy-two thousand! Years and years of accumulated communications! The good news was it was no harder for this client to get to zero (which he did) than for someone with 5000 emails. Both had the same amount of current work to sort through; the former just had a bigger backlog. The key to dealing with the backlog is to do it quickly, like ripping off a band-aid!

If you find yourself in this position, I recommend a three-stage process to get up to date quickly. Mount Rushmore, in the Black Hills of South Dakota, is a wonderful monument to four past presidents whose heads are carved into the rock face (see figure 6.1). But, as detailed as those sculptures are, they were not carved out with chisels—at least not to start with.

They first brought in dynamite and blasted the granite cliff face to create very rough head shapes. They then used

Figure 6.1: can Mount Rushmore help you with your email?
Source: © Critterbiz/Shutterstock

sledgehammers to roughly shape the features. Finally they got out the chisels and started on the fine detail.

Take the same approach with your overflowing inbox. Go back a month in your inbox. Chances are everything before that date is already done or it never needed action in the first place, or it is now so old that it has passed its use-by date. Don't worry, someone would have chased you up already if it was important. This just needs to be moved en masse into one filing folder. Highlight everything before this date and drag it to filing. Create a folder called 'Backlog' if you have to — just get them out of your inbox. That was the dynamite phase.

Now to the sledgehammers. Sort what is left in your inbox by either the *From* or the *Subject* field. Your emails will be grouped in a way that makes it easy to delete or file whole groups of emails that are no longer relevant (distribution-list emails, alerts and non-critical senders).

Finally, sort your emails again by date, and use the chisel approach to process what is left using the four decisions covered in the processing feature at the end of Part II. Backlog sorted!

So many people worry that they will not be able to get on top of their inbox because there are simply too many emails. The Mount Rushmore approach removes that barrier very quickly. If you cannot get to zero in two hours or less, the chances are you will not do it at all. Getting to zero is a reasonably quick task, so don't use time as an excuse. Get up to date, then get your head out of your inbox and into more important work!

Schedule email actions

Get actions out of your inbox and into your centralised action management system.

Emails that require action and are worthy of your time deserve to be managed well. If they are urgent you should deal with them as quickly as possible, sometimes straight away. If they are not urgent, but are a priority and could as well be dealt with at a later time, then they are no longer just emails — they are actions. And they should be treated with the full honour that a priority in your busy world deserves. As discussed in Part I, this means prioritising and scheduling them.

Using your inbox as an action management system just does not cut it any more. It may have worked to some degree when we were getting only a few emails each day, but now that we face a daily torrent of electronic communications, leaving things to be actioned later just creates confusion, stress and a chance that things will slip through the cracks.

So if it is worth doing later, it is worth creating a task or scheduling time in your calendar to do it. As I have said, all the main email and calendar systems allow emails to be actioned and scheduled in this way. Outlook and Lotus Notes allow you to drag an email into the Task or To-do folder to convert it into a task. Outlook even allows you to create dedicated Quick Step buttons in your inbox to convert an email directly into a task or calendar entry. Google Calendar has an Add to Task button in the inbox. All of these functions will copy the email into a task and allow you to set a date and a priority for the action.

Once you have processed the email, and you are comfortable in the knowledge that your action management system will remind you of what you need to do and when you need to do it, you no longer need the email in your inbox. As your 'letterbox' for incoming mail, your inbox should be kept as clear as possible. So the next question should now be, 'Do I need to keep a copy of this for future reference?' If so file it, if not delete it. Either way, *get it out of there*. Move on.

Creating an email actioning system and routinely processing your emails in this way gives you control, creates focus and increases your capacity to do the work in a timely way. Watch your stress levels fall as your control over the work increases.

Be decisive

Make fast decisions when processing your email.

Great leaders are often great decision makers. That applies to the small stuff just as much as the big stuff. They are decisive and know that fast decisions are most often more effective than slow deliberations. This is true for email too. So many messages get stuck in our inbox purely because we looked at it and failed to deal with it immediately, opting to think about it again sometime later. Sometimes we look at the same email again and again before finally dealing with it.

I believe this is a type of procrastination. We scroll through our inbox, trying to remember which emails are still outstanding. We mark emails as unread or flag emails to make the actions more visible, but we are still just shuffling up and down the list. How many times do you touch an email before you actually deal with it? Or do you forget to deal with it at all? So much time is wasted in touching things again and again, which also increases stress. Make decisions. Delete what you don't need to keep, file what you do. Delegate work to others where appropriate. If there is an action needed by you, either do it or schedule time for it. Next stop — Inbox Zero!

Process all your inputs

Manage all forms of incoming work.

As discussed in Part I, not every action that comes your way will arrive as an email. You receive work through a number of different channels. So what strategies can you use to ensure that you stay on top of your total workload and make visible everything that you need to do?

Firstly, identify all of the ways in which work arrives in your world. Here are some common sources of work that need our attention:

- emails in your inbox
- paperwork in your in-tray

- phone and voicemail

- meeting actions captured in your notepad

- thoughts in your head ('mind clutter')

- verbal requests from managers and colleagues

- other system inputs you receive in your role (CRM, approvals and so on).

Make sure you process each of these inputs on a regular basis. Here is an outline of how I manage all of my inputs.

Inbox

I have several different email addresses, but all emails arrive in the one inbox in Outlook, which I process to zero at least once a week, but usually every few days. I routinely turn emails into tasks or schedule them in my calendar to manage the actions.

Paper in-tray

I don't get a huge volume of paper any more, but I do get bills, reports and some letters. These are all placed into my in-tray, which I process every few days. If a call for action arrives on paper, I schedule the task in Outlook, then place the paperwork in a manila folder labelled 'Task paperwork', which sits in a manila file rack on my desk. I note this in the task in Outlook, so I remember where the paperwork is when I go to do the task.

Voicemail

I try to listen to my voicemail messages with a pen in my hand so I can write down messages and numbers. If I cannot return the call then and there, it becomes a task in my task list.

MS Teams posts

MS Teams is being used as a way of collaborating on work, especially with hybrid teams. This means that we are likely to receive delegations and work requests through Teams from time to time. I do not believe that Teams' channels should be used to delegate work, as it is an indirect communication tool (compared to an email which is pushed into your Inbox and therefore is more direct). If you ask me to do something through MS Teams, there is a greater risk that I may not see it, so you are better off sending an email or having a conversation when delegating or requesting work.

That said, it will happen, so what do you do when you receive an action through MS Teams? I reckon the trick is to get the post into your Inbox in Outlook where you won't forget to process and action it. As mentioned earlier, you can send a post as an email to yourself from Teams, which is a nice, neat solution.

Meeting notepad

I have two formats for capturing meeting notes—one low-tech, one high-tech. When appropriate, I capture my meeting notes and actions on my laptop in OneNote, a tool that is a part of the Office suite. This allows me to type my notes, capture my actions and then store them in a fully searchable way. And with the press of a button on my OneNote toolbar, I can also schedule my actions as tasks in Outlook (see figure 6.2).

Sometimes it is just not appropriate to be faffing around with technology while in a meeting. Sometimes the connection with the other people is more important than how the notes are taken. So I also still use a paper notepad for some of my notes, but I ensure these are transferred to Outlook as soon as possible. During the meeting I mark any required actions with

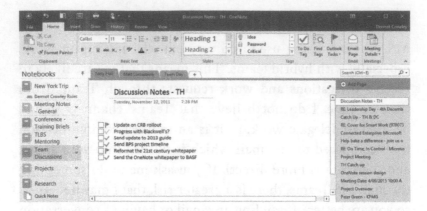

Figure 6.2: OneNote meeting actions

an asterisk, and when I get back to my desk I review my notes and schedule or delegate these actions.

Whichever way I capture the notes and actions, I see the capture tool as just that. It is not the tool by which I manage the action. Everything is centralised in my system if it needs action.

On a final note, you may have other systems that deliver work to you, such as your CRM (customer relationship management) system, a project management system or a bespoke workflow system. These systems are generally designed to manage activities in relation to the customer (or the project), but they rarely manage the work in the context of your time. Your calendar and task list do this, so make sure everything you need to do is centralised.

Tech Tips

Processing your inbox to empty is one of the most liberating and productive habits we can build. But to get to zero on a regular basis, we need to remove any resistance to processing emails.

Here are some tips to help you make your technology work for you.

- Drag emails out of your inbox. Drag them into folders to file them. Drag them to your calendar to schedule time for them. Drag them to your tasks to schedule priorities. In Outlook, left-clicking and dragging will copy the text, and right-clicking and dragging will give you the option of copying or moving the entire email as an action.

- Remove even more friction using Outlook by setting up dedicated Quick Steps in your inbox to convert emails to tasks or calendar appointments. Click on Create New in the Quick Steps pane above your inbox. A personal favourite of mine is a *Create Task* Quick Step that creates a new task and then files the email in my Filing folder! I also have a *Create Appt* Quick Step that will schedule the email into my calendar, which is good for larger chunks of work.

- If an email needs to be discussed with someone else, consider moving it as a discussion item in OneNote (if using Outlook and Office). Right-click on the email and choose *Send to OneNote* from the drop-down menu, or press the *Send to OneNote* button in the ribbon toolbar. It will allow you to choose a notebook and a section to place the email into. You can then store in one place a list of items to be discussed with that person. I have a notebook set up to capture discussion items for each of my team.

- A note on scheduling emails as tasks using mobile tools: in my experience, most mobile apps will not convert emails into tasks. This is a complicated function, so you may just need to leave these emails in your inbox until you are back at your desk.

KEY PRACTICE
Processing

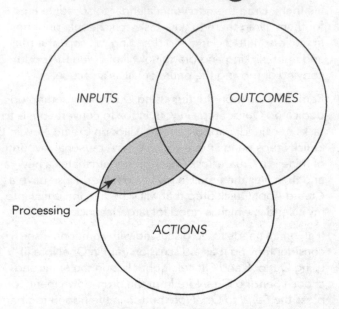

INPUTS

OUTCOMES

Processing

ACTIONS

Figure G: the integrated productivity model—(ii) processing

Processing is the practice that creates a connection between your Inputs and your Actions (see figure G). Processing ensures you are driving the right actions into your action management system, and are filtering out the noise and less important stuff that arrives in your inbox(es) every day.

The decision flowchart in figure H will help you to get your email inbox down to zero. Although this tool focuses mainly on email, it can and should be used to process all of your incoming work down to zero.

Emails are just one form of incoming information, but they are the most prevalent, so we focus here on how to process your emails to zero. In *The 7 Habits of Highly Effective People*, Stephen Covey made famous his version of the priority matrix, a tool for prioritising and making decisions. Many people have

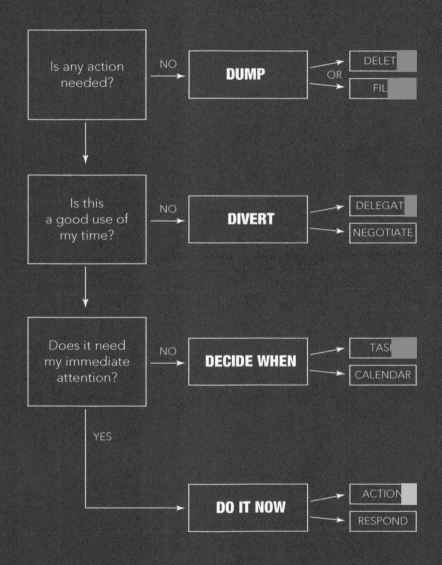

Figure H: email decision flowchart

developed decision-making models based on this framework, with actions usually starting with the letter D.

On the next page, with a big tip of my hat to a great thinker, is my version of the 4 Ds.

The first question to ask yourself when you look at an email is, 'Is any action needed?' If no, then either delete the email or file it, but get it out of your inbox. It serves no purpose there anymore. If the answer is yes, proceed to the next question.

The next question should be, 'Is it a good use of my time?' If not, either delegate it to someone else or negotiate if you will do it or not. Try not to get caught up doing work that is not a good use of your time. This includes accepting low-value meeting invites. If the answer is yes, move on to question three.

Now we are getting to your priorities. The next question is, 'Does it need my immediate attention?' If no, either convert it into a task in your action list or schedule time for it in your calendar. Make a decision about when you will do it. If yes, it should be done immediately, as it is urgent and a good use of your time. Emails like this usually need either a response or an action.

Every single email in your inbox can be processed by asking the questions in this flowchart. You may need to make a double decision about some. You may need to respond to an email and then delete it, or schedule an email as a task and then file it. But if you are decisive, and apply these actions to each email, you will regain control of your inbox and get to zero.

If you manage a group mailbox as well as your personal mailbox, you and your team can use exactly the same strategy to get that to zero. The only additional things you might need to do is to introduce some sort of visual indicator so that everyone in the team knows who is dealing with each email.

Processing is such an important practice that it should become a daily habit, but the time spent processing should be kept to a minimum. You have better things you should be doing! I would personally check my email quickly about once per hour to keep things moving, but I dedicate about 30 minutes each morning and each afternoon to properly process my emails. I then get back to my priorities and meetings.

Hybrid Help: Inputs

Let's have a think about what we need to do differently to manage our Inputs in the hybrid workplace. One of the issues we are now facing is that there can be an increase in the volume of email when we are working in different locations. This is partially due to our need to stay connected with our team, and due to the fact that we no longer have the ability to have what I call 'water cooler conversations'. We used to get so many things moved forward through the impromptu conversations we would have with our colleagues as we passed their desk, or bumped into them on the stairs, outside a meeting room or around the water cooler. So how do we create a virtual environment that allows work to progress quickly without overwhelming everyone's inbox?

Make the cloud your friend

Our technology has really progressed by leaps and bounds over the last few years. When I wrote the first edition of _Smart Work_, tools like Outlook were still very desktop-based, functions like Search were slow and a bit clunky, and it was hard to manage large volumes of information and email filing as we did not have the advantage of storing our information in the cloud.

But a lot has changed now. We can easily access our schedule, task list, emails and documents from any computer, tablet or phone. We can collaborate on documents in real-time with others, wherever they are. We can send links to centralised documents rather than attaching large attachments to emails, thus ensuring that any changes made are reflected in the document rather than having multiple versions of the document flying around. We can visualise projects using project boards, sharing them on everyone's screen in virtual meetings.

But we need to embrace this technology and leverage it. We cannot shy away from it or ignore it, sticking to our old ways and habits. We need to lead by example with our use of technology for the benefit of everyone in our team.

Strive for clarity

We have enough challenges being thrown at us when working remotely without needing the additional challenge of an inbox that is confused and chaotic. Having good habits in place around your email, and all of your inputs for that matter, is crucial. The processing strategy I outlined in the previous section is designed to give you control and clarity.

Be responsive, not reactive

In my book *Urgent!*, I talk about the difference between being responsive and being reactive. There is a world of difference. While I don't recommend that you have email alerts turned on that make you feel like you need to react to every incoming email, I do want you to be responsive to the needs of your team and stakeholders.

Check your email proactively throughout the day and use the SSSH strategy I covered on page 88 to manage expectations if necessary. Consider having a talk to your team to agree on what reasonable response time expectations would be for emails and MS Teams chats. And make sure you carve out some time each day to catch up on MS Teams channel posts and respond as appropriate.

Process your inputs in twenty minutes

In the Hybrid help section at the end of the Actions part, I raised the idea of managing your time using 'thirds' or twenty-minute blocks of time. I suggested that twenty minutes might be the optimal meeting duration, as it is short, sharp and focused.

What if we pushed that idea further and I suggested that there are three 'thirds' or blocks of twenty minutes in an hour, and that maybe when we are working from home or a remote location, we could structure each hour in this way to maximise our energy and attention? We could spend twenty minutes of our hour in a meeting, and spend twenty minutes of our hour processing inputs (see Figure I). That would leave twenty minutes of the hour to focus on our tasks or work that needs our undivided attention.

While it is not realistic to think we could organise every hour in this way, it could be a good strategy for some of the hours in our day. It would ensure that we are being responsive to others, and that we have a better balance between time in meetings and time spent focusing on our priorities.

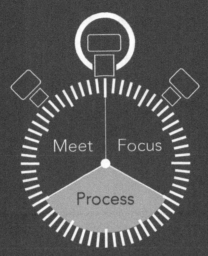

Figure I: managing your time in thirds – (ii) process

Use CC with purpose

When we do not have line of sight over our team and colleagues, it is tempting to copy people into emails more often so that everyone is kept in the loop. But this can result in a massive increase in noise for others, so try to be purposeful in your use of CC.

If you are the sender, and you decide to CC others, the risk is that you may be *over-collaborating*. If you are purposeful in the use of CC, and you think carefully about who really needs to be included, when you copy them, it is a *thoughtful inclusion* that adds value.

If you are a manager that wants to be copied in on everything your team is sending (I see this happen a lot), there is a risk you are *micro-managing*. If you request to be copied in certain things in a purposeful way, I would frame this as *necessary oversight*.

Trust and confidence are key to the effective use of CC. We need to trust our team that they will copy us when necessary, without having to be involved with every email they send, and we need to be confident in our work and ability to prioritise to not copy our manager and stakeholders on every email we send.

PART III
Realise Your
Outcomes

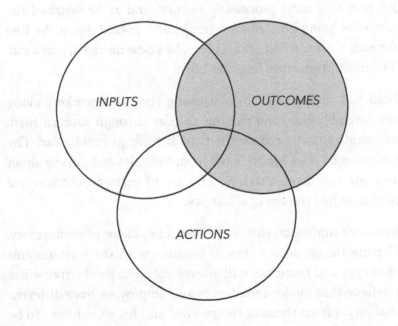

INPUTS

OUTCOMES

ACTIONS

When Henry Ford first introduced the production line in his Model T factory, he popularised efficiency as the key lever to productivity. It was a concept that would shape the industrial workplace in the twentieth century. Efficiency was the key to the success of his Model T motor car, and it changed the way we produced and worked for many decades.

You see, Ford had a problem. The Model T was a car that was an instant hit with the American public — it was simple, handsome and, most of all, reliable. The problem was that he could not make them fast enough. Every car his workforce turned out was sold immediately, and he could not keep up with demand. His teams of specialist workers would work on each car individually, which was labour-intensive and slow. Ford knew that no-one in the auto industry was making cars any faster, so he looked elsewhere for a solution. His research led him to a meat processing factory, and as he watched the carcasses being hoisted onto hooks and passed down the line for each worker to cut off his piece, he knew he had his solution. The mass production line was born.

Ford had realised that by stationing specialist workers along the assembly line, and passing the car through each in turn, he could radically reduce the time it took to build a car. The time to produce a Model T fell from over eleven hours to about an hour and three-quarters. The age of mass production had begun, as had the age of efficiency.

In today's workplace, efficiency is still a key factor in productivity. Getting things done as fast as possible with the least amount of energy and resources will always optimise productivity. But I believe that modern managers and employees have different challenges from those of Henry Ford and his workforce. To be truly productive in the modern workplace we need to work effectively as well as efficiently. We need to make sure we are doing the *right* work efficiently.

To be productive in the Ford factories, efficiency was the key focus because each worker on the production line had only one job. The guy who put the steering wheel on just needed to do that, again and again and again. If Ford could make it easier and quicker for him to perform this role, productivity increased. But in the modern workplace, work has changed, and we no longer have jobs with a single, narrow focus. For the most part we don't simply do the same thing over and over; we do many different things, and we have to make many different choices every day about where we direct our time and energy. So while efficiency has a positive impact on our productivity, I would suggest that effectiveness (the ability to choose the right work to achieve our objectives) creates greater leverage.

This element of decision making is critical to modern productivity. We usually have way more to do than we have time available, which suggests a resource issue. Time is our most limited and valuable resource, and we need to make sure that we are investing it efficiently and effectively — getting the right work done as quickly as possible without compromising quality. Not an easy task when we are bombarded by emails and interruptions, and expected to attend meeting after meeting while working on multiple projects and problems.

Part III focuses on how to spend more of your time on the right work. The first step is to identify your value, and the work you do that really adds value, which is the subject of chapter 7. Then you need to make time to plan, as outlined in chapter 8, and to make sure that you build a planning routine that keeps you organised and focused on the right work. Finally, you need to be able to protect your time. Chapter 9 describes how you can and indeed *must* protect your time from the constant demands of other people as well as from your own procrastination.

CHAPTER 7
Identify your value

American author Henry David Thoreau once said, 'It is not enough to be busy; so are ants. The question is: What are we busy about?' To be truly effective in our work, we need to identify our value, and the activities that will add the most value. We then need to fight for those activities. Fight others who try to steal our time away, and fight our own inertia and procrastination.

I like to think about my work in terms of 'above the line' and 'below the line', a concept I came across in the book *Conscious Leadership*. When I am working above the line, I am working on the things that are a great use of my time. But when I am working below the line, I am getting caught up in work that makes me busy, but does not have impact or value.

Your organisation will probably work with you to help you identify what you need to achieve in your role, and what activities you should focus your time on. This will usually take the form of a performance plan, with goals and objectives, key result areas and key performance indicators (or similar terminology). This should help you to work out what 'above the line' looks like for you. But your performance plan is at risk of being buried in a drawer somewhere, and may see the light of day only twice a year — just before your performance evaluation meeting with your boss.

This chapter looks at some ways you can identify your value and begin to create a real connection between what you are trying to achieve, and what you are doing day to day. It will help you manage the opportunity cost of what you spend your time on. Let me illustrate the issue.

One of my coaching clients was a middle manager in a bank. While he was not a project manager per se, he was involved in a few high-profile projects. One day we were discussing the connection between Outcomes and Actions. He mentioned that he had a couple of critical projects coming up but did not know when he would find the time to focus on them. His schedule was already 'chock-a-block' for the next month.

Reviewing his dense calendar schedule, I asked him how many of those meetings he would count as a 'great' use of his time. With a nervous laugh, he said only a few. When I then asked how they had all made it into his calendar, he sheepishly told me he had accepted the invites himself — he had a case of the 'noddies', as he put it. He had fallen into the trap of doing what everyone else asked him to do, often at the expense of what he really should have been working on. There is always an opportunity cost to everything you spend your time on. The opportunity cost to him was the loss of time to work proactively on his own projects.

Now, of course he would have eventually made time for those projects, but it would have been closer to their deadline, when he was under more pressure and forced to work reactively rather than proactively. This in turn would have put pressure on his team, and continued the cycle of reactivity. This manager quickly learned to be very selective about what he said yes to, as he became more aware of the opportunity costs of those decisions.

Clarify your critical roles

Identify your critical roles and spend 80 per cent of your time working on them.

Our job title often defines our role. Sales Manager, Data Analyst, HR Manager, Team Leader—all of these job titles broadly describe what we do and the area in which we work. But the reality for most of us is that our job is made up of several 'roles', all of which need our time and attention. Indeed, our lives in general are made up of several roles vying for our time and attention.

For example, HR managers manage and lead a team of HR professionals. At the same time, they need to build and manage stakeholder relationships and expectations within the organisation. They might also see the cultural diversity agenda within the organisation as a critical focus. Then add recruitment, talent development, reporting, performance management and any number of other key functions.

The competing pressures of different roles can be overwhelming. It can feel like you are fighting a bushfire with several fronts burning at once. If you are not careful, you end up in reactive mode, jumping from one front to another trying to put out spot fires. One strategy that will help you to work more effectively is to clarify your critical roles and, as a rule of thumb, aim to spend 80 per cent of your time on activities that contribute to these roles. You cannot do everything. By clarifying what is really important you can start to make decisions about what you should and should not focus on.

Project managers among you will know that the *critical path* in a project plan highlights the tasks that are crucial to achieving the project deadlines. Effective project managers will keep a close eye on these tasks, as any delay can have major consequences. To ensure we achieve our goals and objectives, we need to create a connection between our Outcomes and our Actions. I think of this as a critical path between what we are trying to achieve and what we are actually doing on a daily basis.

Conversations with one of my mentors, Matt Church, taught me a valuable lesson about this. Matt is founder of Thought Leaders Global and a world-renowned keynote speaker. At the time, my training business was reasonably successful but had plateaued. No matter how hard I pushed, I could not seem to break through to the next level. I had been in business for ten years and was getting a bit stale. I was not sure that I was committed to the next ten years of doing the same, for the same return. What Matt said to me was instrumental in shifting both my thinking and the focus of my time and attention.

Running a small training business is not complicated, but it does have many elements that need attention. Delivering training and coaching is a part of it, but in the background there are lots of other things to be managed. Financials, marketing, managing the team, social media, blogging, websites, client management, prospecting, reporting — you get the picture. I was busy trying to stay across all of these areas, and did not see any of them as more critical than any other.

Working with Matt helped me to clarify the three BIG roles that deserved 80 per cent of my time and would provide the greatest return on my investment of time (see figure 7.1). For me these roles were creating, selling and delivering. You see, while many things needed my time and attention, the three core areas that added real value to the business were creating and refining my content, getting out there and selling what we do, and of course delivering training and coaching. They were the three

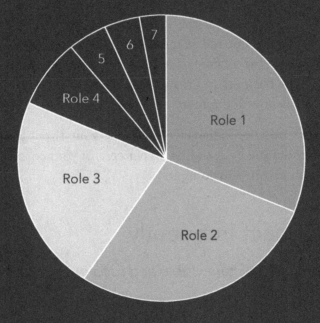

Figure 7.1: what are your three BIG roles?

areas that set my business apart from the competition, built the relationships that help the business to grow and brought money in the door.

While I had been creating, selling and delivering for ten years, I realised the mix was not quite right. I was certainly busy delivering our training and coaching, but I had fallen into bad habits with my sales activity, and did not spend enough time on creating new content. Instead, when I was not delivering, I was focused on all of the lesser roles that seemed to need my time but did not add as much value as creating and selling would. Clarifying where I added value was a lever that not only elevated my business to greater heights but lit the fire for me again. I was now doing more meaningful work and loving it!

I urge you to take some time to clarify your three BIG roles. What should you be spending 80 per cent of your core working hours doing? Are you doing it?

Reconnect frequently

Make the BIG picture visible and reconnect with it often.

When so much of our work is driven by urgency and reactivity, it is easy to fall into the trap of thinking that this constant stream of incoming work is a good use of our time because it is broadly relevant to our roles and is the type of work we think we should be doing. But we need to ask ourselves what the opportunity cost is when we spend so much of our time on this reactive work.

The opportunity cost can be that we are not focusing enough on more important work — work that will directly help us to achieve our goals and objectives. The great work. The problem is, great work is usually not urgent. It is proactive, and because of this we give it a lower priority. It sits in our performance plan, in our project plans or in our head. And we mean to do it. We have the best of intentions, but all too often it just sits there, not getting done. Until, of course, it becomes urgent — and suddenly there we go, reacting again!

To stay focused on the really valuable work, we need to reconnect with the BIG picture frequently. We need to remind ourselves what we really should be doing, and to schedule next-step actions into our action management system so we create traction.

So how often do you connect with your performance plan, and the big picture? Anything less than monthly and you could veer off track. Monthly is good, weekly is better. In the following chapters, we will look at some planning processes that help you to connect with the big picture and schedule the right proactive actions.

Tech Tips

Getting clarity about the most valuable activities that you should focus your time and attention on is essential if you want to maximise your productivity. Keeping these activities front and centre is also essential, as it is so easy to become diverted by bright and shiny distractions.

Here are some ways you can use technology to stay focused on the important stuff.

- When you identify your three BIG roles, set up categories in Outlook to colour-code your meetings and tasks according to these roles. Open an appointment and choose Categorise in the ribbon toolbar. You can tailor the category list by going to All Categories.

- Insert your performance plan as an attached document to an All-Day event in your calendar. Set the start date as the beginning of the year and the end date as December 31. This will mean that the document that should be driving your activities is always just a click away in your schedule. Alternatively, create a page in a OneNote notebook that you review regularly.

- Consider creating project boards in MS Planner to visually capture your longer-term priorities under each of your critical roles. This could create a visual personal dashboard to help you stay focused on the 'above the line' work in your role.

- Schedule recurring appointments for a monthly or weekly review of your performance plan.

CHAPTER 8
Make time to plan

I have found that driving a modern car with built-in sat nav has made me lose my sense of perspective and direction. I get from one place to another by monitoring a screen that shows me the next few hundred metres of the journey, which means my eyes are glued either to the road in front of me or to this tiny screen. Our map books of old were not as functional as a sat nav device, but they did give you a sense of perspective — of where things sat in a wider context.

I think the same is true of our work. We spend our days going from one meeting to another, and in between we are mesmerised by our small screens and incoming emails. It is easy to lose our sense of perspective and of what we are trying to achieve.

Taking time out to plan helps you regain that perspective. Whether you are setting your goals for the year, reviewing progress for the quarter, setting your monthly priorities or planning your week, you are reconnecting with where you are trying to go and how you mean to get there.

Build planning time into your schedule

Make time for personal planning.

Planning increases the quality and quantity of what we get done. Yet when we are busy it is very easy to skip planning and just get stuck into 'doing'. As we know, we need discipline to focus on what we know we should do, even when we might not feel like doing it.

Top athletes have this mindset. They make time to train, and they create detailed plans to achieve their short-, medium- and long-term goals. In business, top performers also have this mindset. They build routines around the important activities that give them that extra productivity.

Former Australian Prime Minister John Howard was famous for his regular morning power-walk in his Australia tracksuit. A TV reporter decided to interview him on one of his walks. One of the questions was on how he found the time in his busy schedule to walk every day. The PM's response was that he did not find the time; he *made* the time, as it was important. That is discipline and a top performer's mindset at work.

In this chapter we will talk about three personal planning processes that you can build into your schedule. They work together to get you organised and focused and, most importantly, to create a line of sight between your Outcomes and your Actions.

Monthly planning

Identify ten big priorities for the month ahead.

While the month ahead will be busy and will involve many priorities, your productivity will benefit from identifying just ten, and then protecting and fighting for time to work on these. Ten is simply a number, but it's a nice round one all the same, and I reckon it makes a good target for the number of big, meaningful 'breakthrough' endeavours to aspire to each month. Ten actions that, if moved forward over the next 30 days, would make a difference. Ten actions you can use as a compass to give you direction in the storm of busyness and urgency you know lies ahead.

I would imagine that right now you could easily identify ten such priorities, although you might keep them buried and inactive. These big-picture priorities are often kept in the back of our minds. We think about them on occasion. We mean to get to them, but they are neglected, pushed aside by our urgent day-to-day work, until they too become urgent. This is often when we take them out and try to find space for them in our busy schedule, adding more pressure and urgency to the mix.

By getting these worthy priorities out of our head and into our schedule early, we begin to balance up the urgent with the important. In his book *First Things First*, Stephen Covey called these proactive priorities 'Big Rocks'. His idea was to get the 'rocks' into your schedule first, and manage the other stuff, the smaller 'stones' and 'sand', around the rocks. Covey writes, 'The key, however, is not to prioritize your schedule, but to schedule your priorities'.

Again, the trick to getting any action done proactively, before it becomes urgent, is to assign the resource of your time to it. That means a next step needs to be scheduled into your calendar or task list, where you can prioritise it and manage it along with your other work. If it stays in your head, you will mean to do it but probably won't get around to it.

Monthly planning is about stepping back to gain some perspective before setting your direction for the next few weeks. When you go on a long hike in the mountains, you need to stop periodically to get your bearings and set your heading for the next leg of the journey. In the same way, you need to reassess your work progress and set a heading for each month. I am sure that without any planning, next month would be extremely busy and full for you. This is your opportunity to balance up the busy work that everyone else demands of you with some meaningful actions that are both aligned to your objectives and important to you in your role.

Sit down (or stand) at the start of the month and write a list of ten things that you would like to move forward this month. They may be projects, deliverables, issues to be resolved, opportunities to explore, decisions to make, personal or work-related. The key thing is they are beyond 'business as usual'; they are what I call *breakthrough actions*. They represent the great work. Once you have your ten, try to rank them in order of most important to least important. Forget about urgency, just assess the value of your spending time on them. What are your top three? These are your starting point, the ones you should fight for and get into your schedule first. For each of the top three, now schedule a next-step action into your calendar or task system to get it moving. Nothing will happen if you just make a list. You must ensure that the list drives your actions — and that means making time for it.

Ensure that over the month you review and update your progress, and ask yourself, 'What is the next step?' Each of your ten meaningful actions should have a next step scheduled into your plan. This is what will create the traction and help you to get the meaningful work done alongside all of the commitments and priorities that make up your 'business as usual'.

The Good, the Bad and the Great

Rate the value of every meeting in your pressured schedule.

How often do you look at the weeks ahead and feel overwhelmed by the number of meetings that you have already booked into your calendar? Where are you going to find the time to get all of those tasks and projects done? Your time has been committed, and it often feels like you are a slave to your calendar — a pawn without any choices.

But this is not true. You should be the one in control of your calendar, because if not, others will be. And when other people control how you spend your time, there is a risk that you will end up very busy, but not necessarily doing the right work — the meaningful work in your role that will help you to realise your outcomes.

In his book *Do More Great Work*, Michael Bungay Stanier writes about doing more great work by doing less good work. Not less bad work, but less *good* work. He suggests that the enemy of 'great' is 'good'. I like this take on work, because it is very easy for us to become complacent doing the good work, convincing ourselves that we are doing our job. But to be truly effective, we need to go beyond requirements. We need to exceed expectations.

If you think back to your three BIG roles, you can probably identify bad, good and great activities in each role (see figure 8.1).

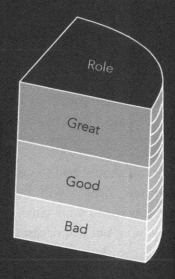

Figure 8.1: bad, good and great work

To force myself to consider the bad, good and great work in each of my roles, each month I do an audit of my meetings and commitments for the month ahead. I call this the Bad, the Good and the Great test (a hat tip to Clint Eastwood's classic western *The Good, the Bad and the Ugly*). Follow these steps to get a really good sense of what you are spending your time on, and free up some lower value time for higher value opportunities.

1. Print out your calendar in a weekly view for the next four weeks.

2. Rate every meeting or commitment in your calendar with an A, B, C or D. Just write the letter on top of the meeting in the printout of your calendar:

   A = Great work — breakthrough activities that are a great use of your time

   B = Good work — business-as-usual work that is classed as 'doing your job'

   C = Bad work — busy work that is not a good use of your time

   D = Don't know — meetings you are attending but don't know why.

3. Make some decisions about each meeting or activity based on the letter you assigned to it:

   A — Protect this time fiercely, and expand it if possible.

   B — Streamline the time spent on this work. Could these meetings be shorter? Could they be handled with a phone call rather than a meeting?

   C — Get rid of this work from your schedule by delegating it to someone else, or dump it altogether if possible.

D—Clarify why you are attending. Re-categorise as A, B or C based on the information. Don't attend meetings if you don't know what you need to achieve or what you need to contribute.

This is a simple but powerful exercise to do once per month. It will give you clarity about what you are spending your time on, and will help you to really focus your time on the right work.

Weekly ROAR planning

Finish each week with a ROAR (Review, Organise, Anticipate and Realign)!

A week is a good chunk of time nicely punctuated by a weekend at either end. It is long enough to get things done but short enough to review and make adjustments if needed. All of which makes it a perfect time frame to build a planning routine around. A weekly routine where you stop, reflect, plan and get set for the week ahead. What I call a weekly ROAR.

Weekly planning for most people is a quick glance at the calendar to get a heads up on the meetings scheduled for next week, and a hurried review of your never-ending task list to see if you have missed anything crucial. The planning and thinking for the week ahead is often superficial, if it happens at all. I call this *one-dimensional planning*. ROAR is a four-dimensional planning process that encourages you to look back, look forward, look up and look all around to consider what needs your time and attention in the next week and beyond.

Weekly planning can be done at any point during the week, but Friday is a sensible day. If you take some time on a Friday to plan the following week, you can close off the week and prepare for the next one. If anything needs to be organised for early next week you still have time. And you can go home feeling that you can let go until Monday and simply enjoy your weekend.

You will need some time and space to plan your week. It is an activity that requires considerable thought and if possible you should protect yourself from interruptions. For most people 30 to 60 minutes is enough time to set aside. This might seem like a lot when you are busy, but remember that by setting aside this time to plan you will get more done. Planning is the type of activity you may procrastinate over if something that seems more urgent comes up, so it is worth scheduling the planning time in your calendar as a weekly recurring appointment. If you have an executive assistant, I highly recommend that you do the weekly planning together so you are both across what needs to happen the following week.

You are ready for your first weekly ROAR! To recap, the four stages of ROAR are: Review, Organise, Anticipate and Realign (see figure 8.2, overleaf).

When planning your week, the first step is to zoom out for a weekly perspective. Go into the week view of your calendar, and open up your task view so you can see the tasks you have scheduled for each day. In this view you can see your workload over the week and move activities around to make it work.

Review

The first step in your weekly plan is to review the week just gone. You need to close off on this week before you can plan the next. Bring yourself up to date, and make sure that any actions left unfinished have been scheduled forward to next week or beyond, or delegated appropriately.

Figure 8.2: ROAR weekly planning process

Firstly, review your meetings from this week and make sure all actions have made it out of your meeting notes. Are there any follow-on meetings that need to be organised? Then review your task list. Are there any incomplete tasks from the week that are not going to get done today? If there are, when are you going to do them? Reschedule as appropriate. Finally, this is a perfect time to clear the backlog and get your inbox to zero! Then you will have a complete picture of what needs your time and attention.

The core review steps are:

1. Review your meetings from the last week for actions.

2. Review your task list, re-prioritise and reschedule.

3. Process your inbox to zero.

Organise

Next, look at the week to come and get it organised. To start with, review your meetings and think about what needs to happen to ensure they are productive. Are they all the best use of your time? Do you have any clashes? Could any of them be shorter? Do you need to schedule any preparation time? Then look at your tasks for each day next week. What are your most critical priorities? Do you have a reasonable balance between your meetings and tasks? Do you need to block out any time in your calendar for work that requires your complete focus without interruption? What else do you need to do next week that is not in the plan yet?

The core organise steps are:

1. Review your meetings for next week.

2. Review and organise your priorities for next week.

Anticipate

Now look forward a few weeks to see what is coming at you down the track. This is an opportunity to get a head start next week on deadlines that may be looming. Do you have any travel coming up? What needs to be organised in relation to that? Are there any major deadlines over the next month? What can you do next week to drive that work forward proactively? Schedule the appropriate next steps. Do you have a busy reporting period or project milestone coming up? This forces you to plan more proactively and ensures you do not leave things until they become urgent before starting them.

The core anticipate steps are:

1. Look ahead to note any upcoming deadlines or events.

2. Look ahead to plan for upcoming travel.

3. Anticipate any proactive activities you should be starting now.

Realign

Remember your top ten BIG priorities list from earlier in the chapter? This may be a good time to review it. Reconnect with the big picture and think about what activities you need to schedule over the next couple of weeks to drive your most important work forward. Review your goals and objectives and ensure the activities you have scheduled for next week are aligned. Think about your different roles and what you need to do in each of those areas. It might also be worth having a think about the key stakeholders in each of these roles and capture the topics you should discuss with them in the coming week or so. Lastly, review any projects and bring them up to date, scheduling any next-step actions that drop from them.

The core realign steps are:

1. Review your objectives and top ten list and schedule next steps.

2. Consider your different roles and identify next steps.

3. Review any projects, update progress and schedule next steps.

The ROAR weekly planning process is a powerful way to finish your week and prepare for next week. I urge you to make the time to do this, as it will surely increase the quality of your results.

Here is a great example of how ROAR helped a team to work more proactively.

One day, when delivering a planning presentation to a financial planning team at their annual three-day retreat, I was interrupted in mid flow by the CEO.

I had been asked to run a session focused on personal planning. I was talking through the ROAR process, and as I discussed the idea of anticipation he jumped up and asked if he could just make a point.

With that, he drew the group's attention to the fact that they had spent the previous day talking about their most strategic actions for the year ahead. One of the critical parts of their role had been identified as 'quarterly reporting'. He made the point that it was called 'quarterly reporting' for a reason — it happened every quarter. Yet every quarter, without fail, they all seemed to run around like headless chickens trying to pull it all together at the last moment. 'This is what we should be doing', he said. 'Anticipating!'

It's not rocket science. We just need to take some time out, look up to see what is coming down the track and plan for it. Another illustration of working proactively instead of reactively.

Tech Tips

Making time to plan means viewing planning as a legitimate use of your time. This time should be scheduled and protected. The problem can be that we give that time away too often so we can 'do' a bit more.

Here are some tips for harnessing your technology to help you protect your planning time.

- Block time out in your schedule for planning, using recurring appointments. Choose a time each week to put aside for weekly planning by scheduling a weekly meeting with yourself. Make it recurring by opening the appointment and clicking on the Recurrence button on the ribbon toolbar.

- Insert a planning checklist into your planning appointment in your calendar. Brainstorm the questions you should ask yourself each month or week to get organised. Create this checklist and refer to it each week when planning. Doctors use checklists, as do pilots. So should we.

- Try to ensure you can access big picture information like your goals and objectives and projects on your mobile devices. That means there is no excuse for not doing your weekly planning just because you are working from home or at another location.

CHAPTER 9
Fight for importance

In his book *The New Rules of Management*, Peter Cook writes about implementing projects that matter. One of the key principles I learned from him is the concept of 'fighting for three'. He writes, 'Fight for three sessions a day of productive work on your big projects. Three 30-minute to one-hour blocks of your best work is much better than 16 hours of responding to requests, shuffling emails, following systems and getting stuff done'.

You, me, Bill Gates, the Pope — we all have the same amount of time in our week. What we do with that time is the critical factor, and how passionately we fight for what is truly important can make the difference.

Make it visible

Get the important stuff out of your head.

If the important things you want to achieve are not in front of you, you can easily lose sight of them and be distracted by the bright, shiny busy work in your inbox. We all have outcomes we want or need to achieve. There are not that many of them, and we know what they are. But we fall into the trap of mentally 'shelving' them, trying just to hold them in our head.

A while back I was working with a senior HR director on his personal productivity. He was a great student and followed everything I suggested. He cleared his full inbox to zero. He simplified his filing system. He set up his calendar and task list and converted from a paper to-do list to electronic tasks.

In our third coaching session together, I posed a simple question. What were his top three priorities over the coming quarter? Without hesitation, he named three major initiatives he was driving forward in the organisation. Great—he had clarity. Then I asked him to show me where in his extremely busy schedule he had put time aside for these three projects over the coming few weeks.

This caught him by surprise and he scratched his head. 'Mmm, they are not in there', he admitted.

He was a fan of Stephen Covey, and we talked about Covey's rocks and sand story, where rocks represented the important priorities in life. I asked him where he thought his 'rocks' were. The penny dropped for him. He then told me excitedly where the rocks were: 'In my head — I have rocks in my head!'

We laughed, but we both knew it was not a laughing matter. As good a student as he was, if he wanted to go to the next level with his productivity he needed to get the rocks out of his head and into his schedule. He needed to make the big stuff visible, and plan his time around it before his busy schedule filled up with everyone else's priorities.

That was a big lesson for him that day, and one that made a real difference to his focus, his results and his stress levels. He printed out a list of his top priorities and projects, and stuck it up on his wall to keep it in his line of vision from that day onwards.

So how do you make your top priorities visible? This will depend on your workplace, and how comfortable you are with making this information public. My advice is to make them as big and visible as possible, so you are regularly reminded of your big priorities. Print out your list in A3 format and stick it up on your wall, as my coaching client did.

Here are some other ideas:

- Use mind maps (created on your PC and/or printed out).

- Keep a digital list in an All-Day Event in your monthly calendar.

- List them on the back page of your notepad.

- Use a dedicated page in OneNote.

The key is that you do the thinking, make this list visible and then look at it regularly to stay focused on the right activity.

Watch out for the procrastination pixie

Don't put off until tomorrow what you should do today.

Procrastination means putting something off until another time, even when you know such a delay may have negative consequences. When it comes to the proactive activities that often help us to achieve our outcomes, it is very easy to procrastinate and miss opportunities, or wind up in a stressed heap as we try to rush through the work at the last minute.

Just recently I fell into the procrastination trap. I had set myself the task of starting a complex white paper that was of enormous value but needed some deep thinking and writing. I had a couple of meetings in the morning and a few emails to send, but I had blocked out some time over the lunch break to work on the writing.

Because I had blocked out the time in my calendar, I stopped what I was doing when the alert popped up, opened the document and set to writing. The first thing I needed was a quote to open the paper. As I searched for a good quote to use, the procrastination pixie came to visit!

Forty-five minutes later I found myself on the floor putting together an office stool I had bought over the weekend. As I screwed on the final leg, it came to me that this was not what I should have been doing. I was meant to be writing the white paper! How on earth had this happened?

As I sat there, I ran through what I had done in the last 45 minutes. Looking for that quote, I'd seen an online post worth reading and commenting on. I realised I needed a coffee, so I popped next door for a takeaway. I then made a quick call, and on hanging up I decided to put together my new stool. All without any conscious awareness that I was procrastinating. It was as though the pixie had taken over my mind and mischievously diverted my attention to less important things. I was honestly gobsmacked by how easily I had been distracted.

We tend to procrastinate over things that are hard, complex, time-consuming or distasteful. It is easy to see that discipline is the essential key to avoiding procrastination, but the following strategies can also help:

1. **If it is complex, break it down.** Spend ten minutes creating a thumbnail sketch of the task. This time spent planning will unlock the complexity and make the task easier.

2. **Block out time in your calendar for this work when doing your weekly planning.** A 'hard' scheduled time helps to focus you on the task at hand and means you are more likely to do it at the appointed time.

3. **Respect your calendar.** Whether you have scheduled a meeting with someone else or blocked out time for yourself, it should not go into your calendar if it is not important. So treat it as important, and avoid getting derailed by urgent reactive work.

4. **Build in accountability by making a public declaration about the work.** Tell a colleague about your plan or agree to a deadline with a stakeholder.

5. **Just get started.** There is a saying among runners that getting your shoes on is the hardest part.

6. **Work out what the blockage is and identify the next thing you could do to unblock it.** Is it the complexity? Ask for help or break it down. Is it the time needed? Just schedule 30 minutes and see how far you get. Is it distasteful? Do it first thing so that everything else in the day feels better. Is it just hard work? Identify a reward and treat yourself when you finish. (I am allowed to have lunch when I finish this chapter — true!)

Blocking strategies

Use your calendar for the really important stuff.

As we discussed in chapter 1, sometimes it is a good idea to 'hard schedule' an activity in your calendar rather than 'soft schedule' it in a task list. Blocking out time in your calendar will help you to focus on more important work in two ways:

1. You will protect time for the work.

2. You will reduce procrastination because you have set a specific time for the activity.

Be careful not to block out everything in your calendar. Because your calendar works best for meetings and fixed work, you will find it too inflexible for many of the smaller tasks you might need to do that are not time-specific. But when used for the few really important things it is a simple and effective strategy.

It is also worth thinking about blocking out time for the following activities to protect your time and reduce procrastination:

- processing emails

- weekly and monthly planning

- project planning or brainstorming

- heading home (your boundaries)

- personal appointments

- reading (newsletters, industry articles, reports)

- thinking.

I really like the last one — thinking time. Wouldn't you like more of that? Wouldn't it improve the quality of your work and life? A senior lawyer I once worked with told me how her boss encouraged the lawyers in her team to look out the window (they had a nice view). Her boss said that if he caught them looking out the window, he knew they would be doing some real thinking, which was what they were paid to do! We need more of that.

Delegate early and well

Make time for the important by letting go of other work.

In their roles as productivity trainers and coaches, people in my team often hear people joke that they don't need to be more organised — they need a 28-hour day!

The fact is, time is the most precious and limited resource you have. The best time managers tend to manage their work according to a simple but powerful principle: in order to focus on the most important work, you need to let go of the less important work. Every time you devote time and energy to something that is not a good use of your time, you are denying this resource to other, more important work. So how do you get rid of the lower value work that comes your way each day? One underutilised strategy is to *delegate*.

Now most of us do delegate some of our lower value work by necessity, but we also often hold on to work that could be delegated. We hold on because we don't have faith in the outcome if we hand it to someone else and we want to maintain control, especially of more complex, higher risk work. The following section will look at the *why, what, when, who* and *how* of delegating work effectively, as well as strategies for maintaining the appropriate amount of control over the work.

Why delegate?

For managers, professionals and supervisors, delegation is critical to achieving goals and objectives in a balanced way. The opportunity cost of not delegating effectively is that you don't get to the work that is the best use of your time — unless, of course, you are happy to work longer hours. I see it time and time again: managers working unnecessarily long hours to keep across everything. Effective, clear and timely delegation can help spread the load and maximise the use of all the resources in a team.

Delegation is also a great way of growing the skills of the team. Delegating work to others forces them to step up and work at a higher level. Over time, as their experience grows, you can delegate more complex work to them, leveraging your time to focus on other work.

What to delegate?

Every day a constant stream of work flows our way. Much of it is directed to us because we are the appropriate person to deal with it, but some of it comes to us with the expectation that we will organise someone else to do it. This is work that we should, wholly or partially, delegate to others within the team or within our sphere of influence.

When work is directed to you, first ask yourself whether this is a good use of your time? If it is work that needs to be done but is not a good use of your time, delegate it. (If it is of little value, consider dumping or deleting it.) Even if you cannot delegate the whole task to someone else, consider delegating a part of it and finishing the task yourself. For example, you may be able to delegate the drafting of a report, which you can then review and put the final touches on.

When to delegate?

As soon as possible! Too often I see people who do not manage their incoming work well and end up leaving emails in their inbox for a week until they become urgent. If you put off delegating the work until then, you are asking for trouble. Work delegated at the last minute just transfers the pressure to someone else, leading to mistakes and resentment.

By delegating work in a timely way, you will avoid bottlenecks, and make it easier for your team to do their work well. It will also give you more time to check on the quality of the work and jump in and help if necessary.

Who to delegate to?

First of all, you turn to whoever you have within your sphere of delegation influence. This often means your team and support staff, but could also involve people in other teams, external contractors or consultants, or project team members who may not directly report to you. Ask yourself this question: Who is the person best placed to do this?

Within the group of possible people to delegate to, you need to consider who is the best fit for the job. Who has the skills or knowledge to do the job well? Who has the capacity to do the work in the time frame? Who would find the work stimulating? Whose skills do you need to grow in this area?

How to delegate the work?

We often most need to delegate when we are busy, but when we are busy we tend to take shortcuts and delegate poorly. A little time spent delegating clearly will save time in the long run. Here are some pointers to help ensure effective delegation:

- Delegate face-to-face when possible. This allows you to check for understanding and provides room for questions and negotiation.

- Consider the complexity/risk involved in the task, and the experience of the person to whom you are delegating the task. (See the delegation matrix in figure 9.1.)

- Clearly outline what needs to be done, by when, to what level of quality and what your expectations are about reporting and decision making. In what circumstances should they check with you before proceeding?

- Check what capacity they have to do the work in the required time frame. There is no point further overloading an already overworked resource. Allow them room to negotiate.

- Leave them to it, but check on progress at the agreed times. Don't micromanage as it just slows them down and increases pressure.

- Schedule a 'Track it back' task to remind you when to expect the work.

The delegation matrix

A useful framework when choosing the best way to approach delegation and progress reporting is the delegation matrix (see figure 9.1), which takes into account the risk and complexity involved with the work, as well as the experience of the person completing it.

The decision you make about who to delegate to and how closely you need to manage the delegation can be facilitated by using the delegation matrix:

High Risk/High Experience. In this situation, it is critical that the work is done well and on time, but you are confident of the skills and experience of the person completing the work.

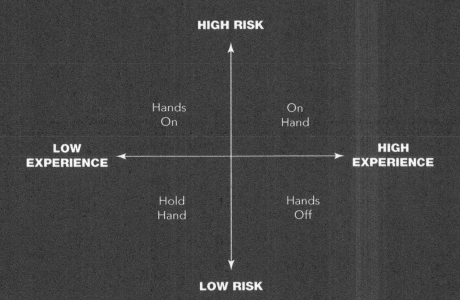

Figure 9.1: the delegation matrix

Use an 'on hand' delegation style, working in
partnership to decide on the best way to do the work, and
keep a reasonable level of input to ensure the quality of
the final product. Regular updates should be scheduled,
and clear guidelines put in place about what decisions need
approval by you.

High Experience/Low Risk. In this situation there is less
risk or impact if something goes wrong or there is a delay,
and you are confident of the skills and experience of the
person delegated to do the work.

Use a 'hands off' delegation approach. Delegate the
work quickly but clearly, and set the expectation that no
reporting is necessary unless there is a major issue or delay
that needs your input to resolve. You trust the ability of
the person completing the work and their capacity to solve
any problems themselves. Using email to delegate may be
appropriate here.

Low Risk/Low Experience. There is less risk or impact if
something goes wrong or there is a delay, but you are also
less confident of the skills and experience of the person
completing the work.

Use a 'hold hand' delegation style, guiding and helping,
but allowing the person completing the work to think
for themselves. You might encourage them to come up
with some options for how they would approach the task
and then advise on which you feel is the best approach.
Because there is less risk here, it is a great opportunity
to increase their skills and confidence. Only moderate
reporting is necessary, and once you have delegated you
may just need a heads-up when it is complete, or if there is
an issue or delay.

High Risk/Low Experience. In this situation it is critical that the work is done well and on time, but you are less confident of the skills and experience of the person delegated to do the work.

Use a 'hands on' delegation style, providing clear instructions on what needs to be done, how it should be done and the deadline. You could get them to do a piece of the work and then come back for further instructions. The key here is regular check-ins to monitor progress and to make adjustments when needed.

Whatever your role, think about how much you delegate currently and how effectively you delegate that work. Look for ways to delegate more work where appropriate, keeping in mind the workload of others. This is not a strategy for dumping unwanted work on others, but an opportunity to maximise your time and leverage the resources around you.

Tech Tips

Time is your most precious resource. Protect it fiercely and harness the power of technology to protect it for you. Here are some ideas on how to do that.

- Make the big picture visible by creating a mind map of your strategic roles, priorities and projects using one of the many mind-mapping software tools available for your desktop, tablet or smartphone. A mind map provides a clear, concise picture of your work that can help you to stay connected with what is important.

- Delegate tasks electronically using the Assign Task function in Outlook or Lotus Notes. This allows you to assign an action but still retain visibility of the progress. Be careful, though; while it might be efficient, assigning a task is not always the most effective way to delegate work.

- Reduce procrastination by scheduling time for your most important work. Block it out in your calendar, or at least schedule a high-priority task for the appropriate day. Make it visible in your system, and see yourself as your most important customer!

- Use MS Planner or a similar tool to plan and manage projects in a simple way. Attach these plans as a Tab to MS Teams channels so that they are close at hand when you are discussing and collaborating online with your team.

KEY PRACTICE
Planning

INPUTS

OUTCOMES

Planning

ACTIONS

Figure J: the integrated productivity model—(iii) planning

The final core practice we need to examine is planning. Time spent planning not only gets you organised but creates a critical path between your Outcomes and your Actions (see figure J). It ensures you are not just getting caught up in busy work but are doing the *right* work.

We have already looked at three planning routines to create this critical path. Monthly planning helps you to step back and get perspective. Weekly planning gets you organised, and daily planning keeps you focused and creates traction.

We have also talked about getting clear on what the big picture looks like for you. Setting objectives, defining your three core roles, identifying projects and priorities to focus on to achieve these. Fighting for time to work on activities that progress these and help you to achieve your goals and objectives. Let's now bring all of that together in one cohesive framework for personal planning (see figure K, overleaf).

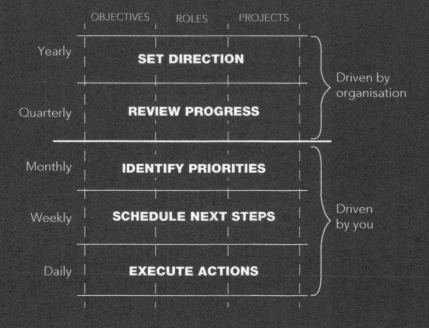

Figure K: personal planning framework

'Organisation'-driven planning

You most likely already have in place a range of planning processes to help you to define your roles and focus on the right activity. These will likely take the form of a yearly performance planning process and either a half-yearly or a quarterly review with your manager. I will assume that these are already established and will not interfere with the organisational processes. But how do you create a connection between these processes and what you do on a day-to-day basis?

'You'-driven planning

While we all spend lots of time planning on a team, divisional or even organisational level, most of us do not spend enough time on personal planning. That is the missing link. Anything planned at the conceptual level, and captured in lists (read high-level piles), is just a wish list. And to make it worse, often this planning is framed in terms of objectives we need to achieve rather than actions we need to complete. You cannot leave objectives hanging without an action!

- *Monthly* planning should help you to clarify the big priorities and projects you need to focus your time and attention on in the coming month. The clarity you get from this will help you to execute those actions, but also to prioritise your time and negotiate competing priorities.

- *Weekly* planning will help you get up to date then plan how and when you are going to get everything done. Weekly planning results in your scheduling the right next-step actions that will move your meaningful work forward. If monthly planning is about strategic alignment, weekly planning is about the tactical game plan.

- *Daily* planning is all about focus and execution. What do I need to get done today? What are my priorities? What is realistic? What do I need to reschedule? This is what creates traction and keeps things moving forward. Plan your work and work your plan!

So your planning, from yearly to daily, should be consciously aligned, with each level of planning serving a specific purpose. It should serve to clarify, prioritise, filter, focus, align and execute your most important work. It is well worth building routines around planning. No, it is *critical* to build routines around planning.

Hybrid Help: Outcomes

One of the good things about coming together in a workplace or an office is that it gives us some structure. Being close to our manager and having regular conversations with our team keeps our work moving forward, and helps us to avoid procrastination. When we work remotely the risk is that we lose that sense of structure, and can therefore lose our focus on what is important. To avoid this, we need additional strategies to stay focused on the right things.

Plan your week with location in mind

David Allen, the author of *Getting Things Done*, champions a task management approach driven by contextual lists. One of the key contexts he uses is location. So, he creates lists of things that can be done when in the office, or when online, or when on a plane.

I have never been a huge fan of this approach, believing that organising your tasks by date is more proactive and action focused. That said, I can now see the value in bringing locational contexts into your thinking when you are planning your week.

As you do your weekly planning (see the Weekly ROAR in chapter 8), consider how you can best spend your time given the different locations you might be working from. If you will be in the office, what are the meetings you could organise that would best be served by being face-to-face with the other participants? What conversations would you like to have with colleagues when you are there, and do you need to make a list of discussion items in OneNote? If you will be working from home on Thursday, what tasks might be best scheduled for that day so you have a better chance of getting some focus time away from office distractions.

We have a great opportunity to create a week that is highly productive, but we need to be intentional and organised about it if we are to reap the benefits.

Make your projects visible

When you are not visible to your team, and they are not visible to you, it is even more critical that the work that you are collaborating on as a team is visible to both you and the team. Project work cannot be managed effectively if it is buried in your head, in your Inbox or in an Excel spreadsheet.

Encourage your team to learn to use tools like MS Planner to make the project activities visible, and track progress regularly as a team using this simple project board tool. When you have virtual meetings, have someone share the project board so that you can all see it and talk to it. Use these project boards as a part of your weekly planning and schedule any relevant next step actions into your calendar or task list. (I often get asked if you should use Outlook tasks or Planner tasks to manage your day-to-day actions. I believe that Planner is best used for projects, and will usually contain larger chunks of work. The task list in MS Outlook is designed to help you to manage your time, so is the better tool for day-to-day activities. Typically the actions that go into your Outlook task list are more granular next-step actions.)

Plan time to focus using Thirds

In sections one and two I raised the idea of mentally dividing an hour of your time into three blocks of twenty minutes, or what I call 'Thirds'. This is not meant to be a literal concept every hour, but a useful mindset around how you distribute your time.

If twenty minutes of your hour was spent in a meeting with others, and twenty minutes of your hour was spent processing inputs, the final twenty minutes of your hour should be spent focusing on important priorities (see Figure L).

As mentioned in section one, I can get significant things done or progressed in twenty minutes. I am confident that I can either *start*, *sort* or *send* any piece of work in that time. I may not be able to complete a larger piece of work, but I could get it started and get the ball rolling. I can get smaller tasks sorted and ticked off of my list, or I can get something sent to the next in line, moving work forward at a steady pace.

Try not to make work bigger than it is. Some tasks seem to be so big that we need to put aside hours to get them done, and we invariably don't have hours available, so we procrastinate. But often they just need a focused twenty minutes to get some forward movement and momentum.

Strategies like this are key to working effectively in a remote situation, where you need to be more self-driven than in a traditional workplace.

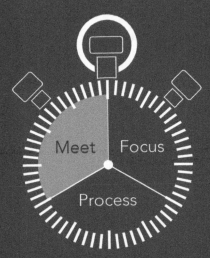

Figure L: managing your time in thirds – (iii) meet

Next steps

Well done, you're still here. You may have flicked to the back, but most of you will have read through the whole book! Either way, what are you going to do next? Are you going to put this book down and go back to your overflowing inbox and business as usual, or are you going to make some changes?

Changing habits and embedded behaviours is never easy. It takes discipline and determination, but the rewards are worth the effort. I have worked with many thousands of people over the past decade, and have formed a view not only on the phases they tend to go through as they adopt the new system, but also on the key things that the successful ones do and don't do in the initial weeks and months after their training. I believe the framework I have developed from this experience, and have outlined in *Smart Work*, will be valuable to all who read this book and decide to put the system in place for themselves.

When we learn a skill, whether by reading a book, attending a course, or participating in coaching or mentoring, it takes time and effort to develop the set of habits needed to implement the skill in an ongoing way. Figure M (overleaf) outlines the four phases that I believe you will go through on your way to achieving mastery.

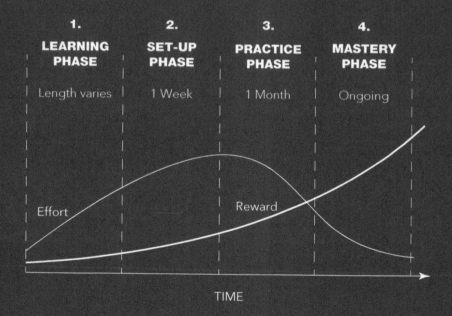

1. **LEARNING PHASE**	2. **SET-UP PHASE**	3. **PRACTICE PHASE**	4. **MASTERY PHASE**
Length varies	1 Week	1 Month	Ongoing

Effort

Reward

TIME

Figure M: the learning mastery curve

You will find you need to invest the greatest amount of effort in the first weeks after the initial learning phase, but with practice the effort required will moderate and level off. At the same time, the rewards will increase over time. The key is to be patient and not to give up before you reap the benefits of your new habits and skills.

The learning phase

This is the time you invest in learning a new skill. You might learn it through attending a course — or by reading this book. Either way, you will discover a new way of doing things and will hopefully be inspired to make fundamental changes to your work life. I have summed up the *Smart Work* approach in these words: *centralise your actions, organise your inputs and realise your outcomes.* You needed to invest some effort in reading this book and thinking about the concepts, but the reward is still low for you. To increase the reward, you need to move into the set-up phase.

The set-up phase

Your productivity is not going to increase just because you have read a book or attended a course. You now need to *do something.* And the starting point is setting up your system so you can begin to implement your new skills. These are the core processes you need to focus on in the set-up phase:

- Centralise all of your actions using one tool, such as Outlook, and commit to a centralised way of working.

- Set up a forward schedule view in Outlook for both meetings and tasks.

- Set up a simple filing system for emails.

- Clear your inbox to zero.

- Set up rules to reduce your email noise.

- Schedule time for your daily, weekly and monthly planning routines.

- Clarify your three big roles and your objectives.

- Set up your mobile tools to sync fully with Outlook.

This phase should be completed within a week, because if it becomes too drawn out you lose momentum. The effort levels are high here and you may not yet be seeing a reward, but hang in there. Practice will begin to reduce the effort and increase the reward.

The practice phase

Now you need to practise using this new system. I believe that if you do some simple things consistently for four weeks you will begin to form some solid new habits. This is where you need to be disciplined and to make a real effort to use your new skills. Here are some pointers on what to practise:

- Practise scheduling your priorities in your calendar or task list.

- Be decisive when checking your email.

- Process to zero once a week for four weeks.

- Start each day with a daily plan.

- Plan your week four times over the next month.

You should begin to see the amount of effort you need to put in diminish, and you'll start to enjoy the rewards. Now, on to mastery!

The mastery phase

A friend of mine has a black belt in Aikido. That means he is very, very good at that discipline. But in his mind he is still a novice, and he spends much time each year learning, practising and meditating on the path to becoming a master. Mastery takes lots of time and practice, but in the mastery phase the rewards outweigh the effort you put in.

So keep practising until you achieve mastery. If you fall off the wagon, get up and get back on again. If work pressures mean you let your new skills go for a while, that's okay. When you come up for air, refocus and get back to working productively. A master knows when to maintain strict discipline and when to let go.

Our workplace will continue to change, as will the productivity challenges we are faced with. But I believe that the Smart Work approach will remain evergreen, and can help you to stay focused and balanced wherever, and however you work.

I wish you all the luck in the world in putting your new system in place. Now, over to you. Let the Smart Work begin!

Index

adapt

Thank you for reading *Smart Work*. I hope it has provided some insights into how you can adapt to the challenges of the 21st century workplace. But now it is time to implement!

When I am not writing books (which is most of the time), myself and my team work with organisations to help their people to implement the concepts outlined in *Smart Work*. If you feel that one of our speaking, training or coaching offerings could help your team, get in touch through our website and let's have a conversation!

www.adaptproductivity.com.au

I love connecting, so feel free to connect with me on LinkedIn or email me on dermot.crowley@adaptproductivity.com.au

Until next time...

Dermot